INTRODUCTION: The McDonnell Douglas C-9 was a military version of the extremely successful McDonnell Douglas DC-9 airliner. It was produced as the C-9A "Nightingale" and VC-9C VIP transport for the United States Air Force, and the C-9B "Skytrain II" for the United States Navy and Marine Corps.

The C-9A ceased operations in September 2005, the VC-9Cs were retired in September 2011, the Navy C-9Bs quit flying in July 2014, and the two Marine C-9Bs ceased service in April 2017.

CHRONOLOGICAL HISTORY OF THE USAF C-9A NIGHTINGALE 1963-2001 (Provided by the Office of History, Air Mobility Command, Scott AFB and compiled by Cadet 1st Class Janene L. Drummer and Ms. Kathryn A. Wilcoxson):

The C-9A was a twin-engine, T-tail, medium-range, swept-wing jet aircraft used primarily for the Air Mobility Command's aeromedical evacuation missions. It was the first jet aircraft specifically designed for the movement of litter and ambulatory patients. This flying hospital replaced the C-118 "Liftmasters" and C-131A

"Samaritans" as well as the C- "Hercules" and C-141 "Starlifters" the Air Force's primary means medical transportation and evac tion.

The C-9A was fitted with special equipment including a hydraulically operated folding ramp for patient handling; with ceiling receptacles for securing intravenous bottles; a special care area with a separate ventilation system for patients requiring isolation or intensive care; vacuum and therapeutic oxygen outlets; an electrical system for the use of cardiac monitors, respirators, incubators, and infusion pumps; a medical refrigerator for whole blood and biologicals; commercial airline-type seats for ambulatory patients; a special control panel to allow the crew director to monitor cabin temperature, therapeutic oxygen, and the vacuum system; and an auxiliary power unit.

The C-9A could cruise at speeds in excess of 500 mph for a range of 2,000 miles. It carried a maximum of 40 litter or 40 ambulatory patients, as well as multiple combinations of both. A normal crew consisted of a flight crew of three (pilot, co-pilot, and flight mechanic) and a medical crew of five

ed-
ots
:ott
ran
two months and included three weeks of ground school and six days of simulator training. Nurses and aeromedical technicians attended the USAF School of Aerospace Medicine at Brooks AFB, San Antonio, TX. They received six weeks of didactic and "hands-on" training. The courses provided the fundamental skills necessary to operate as aeromedical crewmembers in any USAF aeromedical evacuation aircraft.

21 C-9As were purchased. They were: 67-22583-586, 68-8932-935, 68-10958-961 and 71-0874-882.

APRIL 1963: The Office of the Secretary of Defense requested a modernization study of the aeromedical evacuation fleet. The Fokker/Fairchild Hiller F-27 and Douglas DC-9, or equivalent, were

Below, first Air Force C-9A, S/N 67-22583, under final construction at Douglas in May 1968. (Harry Gann via Paul Minert collection)

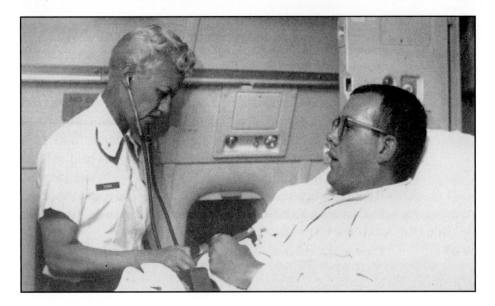

suggested. The F-27 was rejected, despite being less expensive. An updated study was to be resubmitted after 1 July 1965.

JUNE 1964: As a follow-up to the submittal of April 1963, the Military Air Transport Service (MATS) continued to provide updated information to Headquarters USAF and presented a briefing that re-emphasized the urgency of aeromedical modernization needs. The presentation pointed out the deficiencies and existing limitations of the current airlift capacity and frequency of service. MATS stressed the need for a medium-weight jet aircraft with adequate space, weather radar, and modernized very high frequency (VHF) communications.

15 APRIL 1965: The findings and recommendations of MATS, together with Headquarters USAF revisions, were published in the form of a comprehensive study. However, no replacement for the C-131A followed.

16 MAY 1966: The Special Subcommittee on Military Airlift of the Committee on Armed Services of the House of Representatives recommended the immediate modernization of the fleet by acquiring an Air Force-recommended jet aircraft, such as the DC-9 or the Boeing B-737. A jet aircraft would reduce costs and increase efficiency over propeller-driven aircraft for intratheater missions.

29 JULY 1966: The Department of Defense (DOD) agreed to initiate modernization in January 1967 and approved the expenditure of $34 million for the purchase of 8 aircraft plus initial spares.

FALL 1966: Competition for the contract began. Known as the CX-2 Program, requirements for the aircraft were as follows: it must be capable of operating under extreme climatic temperature and humidity conditions and be operationally independent of ground support; it must have a cruise speed of Mach .75 or higher and a cruise altitude of 30,000-35,000 feet, with a guaranteed range of 2,000 nautical miles; and it must be capable of carrying 40 ambulatory or 30 litter patients, or a combination of both.

31 AUGUST 1967: The Air Force awarded a $28.7 million dollar contract for the off-the-shelf DC-9 aircraft to McDonnell Douglas Aircraft Corporation, Long Beach, CA. The contract called for 8 C-9As to be delivered, beginning in August 1968, at the rate of one per month. The total was later changed to 12 aircraft before a final total of 21 aircraft was chosen. The contract also called for Medical Suitability Testing to ensure a standard and aeromedically accept-

---

Above left, LCOL Mary Ann Tonne, Chief Nurse of the 375th AAW, Scott AFB, IL, taking a patient's blood pressure aboard a C-9A. She is credited with naming the C-9A "Nightingale". (USAF) Below, roll-out display of the second C-9A, S/N 67-22584, at Douglas Long Beach, CA, on 17 June 1968. Note "Nightingale" on the nose. (Harry Gann)

able interior.

The normal basing was 13 aircraft at Scott AFB, IL, while Pacific Air Forces at Clark AB, PI, and USAF Europe, Rhein-Main AB, Germany, each with 4 aircraft.

20 OCTOBER 1967: Medical Suitability Testing began at McDonnell Douglas, Long Beach. Participants included several civilians, enlisted men and officers testing various areas of the aircraft.

18 JANUARY 1968: A static display of the C-9A was assembled for the 50th Anniversary of Aerospace Medicine at Brooks AFB, TX.

17 JUNE 1968: McDonnell Douglas Aircraft hosted the C-9A rollout ceremonies. Major General Harry E. Goldsworthy, Commander of the Air Force Systems Command's Aeronautical Systems Division, Wright-Patterson AFB, OH, accepted the C-9A from Donald Douglas, Jr., President of Douglas Aircraft Division. LCOL Mary Ann Tonne, Chief Nurse of the 375th Aeromedical

Airlift Wing, Scott AFB, IL, named the C-9A the Nightingale. The name came from Florence Nightingale, a British nurse who pioneered improved military nursing during the Crimean War. While C-9A 67-22583 conducted a fly-over, 67-22584 emerged from a flightline hangar. Elsie Ott Mandot, who in January 1943 during WWII was the first nurse to fly transcontinental with patients (and for this received the Air Medal), christened the aircraft.

10 AUGUST 1968: The first operational C-9A, S/N 67-22584, landed at Scott AFB, piloted by the commander of the Military Airlift Command, GEN Howell M. Estes, Jr.

2 OCTOBER 1968: The first C-9A operational mission was completed on this date. Carrying patients from North Central and Rocky Mountain areas, the twin-engine jet departed from Scott AFB for stops at Buckley Field, CO, Travis AFB, CA, and Kelly AFB, TX. The aircrew completed the mission that night, compared to the two days it would have taken when flying older aircraft.

Above, R.G. Smith promotional illustration for the C-9A in MAC markings. (via Harry Gann) Bottom, the first USAF C-9A, S/N 67-22583, in flight over Southern California in June 1968. (Harry Gann)

20-21 MAY 1969: The C-9A flew its first combination aircrew route familiarization and offshore introduction mission. The mission transited NAS Guantanamo Bay, Cuba; Kindley AB, Bermuda; Ramey AFB, PR; and Howard AFB, Panama.

JUNE 1969: BGEN Harold F. Funsch, MAC Surgeon, led a 16-man crew on a C-9A tour through Europe. The aircraft reaped praises from more than 1,200 medical and flight personnel. Static displays were held at Rhein-Main AB, Furstenfeldbruck AB, Wiesbaden AB and Stuttgart, Germany; Naples, Italy; and Supreme Headquarters Allied Powers Europe near Brussels, Belgium.

NOVEMBER 1969: Four pilots reached the 1,000-hour mark in the

375th AAW

HELP FROM ABOVE

At right, the 375th Aeromedical Airlift Wing was the first unit to receive the C-9A. Note placement of 375th AAW on the C-9A's nose on S/N 68-10959. This aircraft flew the last scheduled C-9A aeromedical evacuation mission on 11 August 2003. (Harry Gann) Bottom, 375th AAW C-9A, S/N 68-8932, landing in 1972. (Harry Gann)

C-9A. Majors John W. Chancey, Roland E. Martin, Henry R. Parnell, Jr., and George G. Banks each received a Certificate of Achievement for logging over 1,000 hours in the "Flying Hospital Ward".

31 MAY THROUGH 8 JUNE 1970: One 375th Aeromedical Airlift Wing C-9A flew its first scheduled missions to Puerto Rico; Guantanamo Bay, Cuba; Goose Bay, Labrador; and

Torbay, Newfoundland. The crew flew an entire route in one day, a mission that took previous aircraft three to five days to accomplish.

19 NOVEMBER 1970 THROUGH 9 SEPTEMBER 1971: The C-9A aircraft established a new Air Force record of 1,282 consecutive on-time home station departures during this period.

21 DECEMBER 1970: McDonnell Douglas delivered the first of a new buy of nine C-9As to the Air Force. Deliveries continued through September 1972. As of this date, the average monthly operational readi-

ness rate, from the inception of service, was 90.8 percent, according to Air Force figures.

23 MARCH 1971: A C-9A set a new military record for the number of patients moved in one day, a total of 96 persons, (24 litter patients, 64 ambulatory patients, and 8 non-medical attendants).

27-28 MARCH 1971: A C-9A commanded by LCOL Neil Leeper airlifted Dr. Claude Fly, the American agricultural advisor to Uruguay released by terrorists after he experienced a heart attack while in captivity. The move was from Charleston AFB, South

Carolina, to Francis E. Warren AFB, WY.

21 APRIL 1971: Military Surgeons General of armed forces from many countries traveled aboard a C-9A from Cleveland, OH, to Colorado Springs, CO. During the flight they were briefed on the aeromedical evacuation mission.

6 JUNE 1971: Reservists from the 932nd Aeromedical Airlift Group, Scott AFB, IL, completely manned aeromedical evacuation mission 1137. Previously, only mixed crews of reservists and active duty personal had flown missions.

JULY 1971: C-9A, S/N 67-22585, became the first C-9 to log 5,000 flying hours.

16 SEPTEMBER 1971: One aircraft, S/N 67-22586, was lost in a crash near Scott AFB on 16 September 1971 during a training mission. The

three pilot crewmembers, LCOL Lloyd M. Clore, MAJ Aubrey L. Akin, and Capt James L. Rhame, died in the crash. This was the first fatal accident both in the history of the C-9A as well as in the 23-year history of the 375th Aeromedical Airlift Wing.

15. MARCH 1972: The C-9A flew its first operational mission in Southeast Asia.

7 JULY 1972: A C-9A transported Alabama Governor George C. Wallace from Andrews AFB, MD, to Montgomery, AL, and to the Democratic National Convention in Miami, FL. Wallace had been partially paralyzed by a would-be assassin's bullet while campaigning in a Laure, MD, shopping center on 15 May.

29 JANUARY 1973: GEN Lucius D. Clay, Jr., Commander in Chief of Pacific Air Forces, approved the use of the C-9A for South Vietnam evacuations.

Above, 375th AAW C-9A, S/N 68-8935, takes off from Andrews AFB, MD, during an air show in 1976. (USAF) Bottom, MAC C-9A, S/N 71-0875, assigned to the 374th TAW. This particular C-9A participated in the repatriation of POWs from Saigon to Clark AB in 1973 and it recovered survivors of the C-5 crash at Tan Son Nhut in April 1975. (NMUSAF via Don Jay)

4 APRIL 1973: C-9As participated in Operation Homecoming, a mission based upon the premise that each returning prisoner of war from Vietnam would require individual medical attention. The aircraft's hospital-like environment controlled their transition from captivity to a free society by permitting a graduated return. The C-9As transported 367 returnees to medical facilities near their families.

10 FEBRUARY 1974: A C-9A from

374 TAW

Above, 374th Tactical Airlift Wing C-9A, S/N 71-0875, out of Clark AB, PI, while assigned to the 20th Aeromedical Evacuation Squadron on 17 April 1979. (USAF) Bottom, MAC C-9A, S/N 68-8934, from the 375th AAW at Kelly AFB in February 1980. (Richard Frank via Phillip Friddell)

the 375th Aeromedical Airlift Wing airlifted the crew of the National Aeronautics and Space Administration (NASA) Skylab IV mission from San Diego, CA, to Houston, TX, after the crew had finished spending 84 days in space on 8 February.

21 FEBRUARY 1974: A C-9A piloted by LCOL Jack B. Compton, 11th Aeromedical Airlift Squadron commander, made the 100,000th aircraft landing recorded at Buckley ANGB, CO. Colorado's lieutenant governor and other dignitaries met with Compton after the mission.

FALL 1974: Personnel from the 375th Aeromedical Airlift Wing Operational Training Division collaborated with operational training personnel from Headquarters MAC on a proposal for the installation of a six-axis visualator for C-9A pilot training at Scott AFB. That same year, Flight Safety International, a private company based at Long Beach, CA, that had provided simulator training to the

375th since 1968, submitted a proposal for a C-9A visualator to be installed in the Scott AFB area. This simulator would reduce training flight hours, freeing the airplanes to fly more operational missions.

25-26 FEBRUARY 1978: In two urgent C-9A missions, the 11th Aeromedical Airlift Squadron and the 57th Aeromedical Evacuation Squadron crews airlifted 14 burn casualties from a train derailment disaster at Waverly, TN. The train had derailed as a result of a propane rail tank explosion. The C-9A transported the burn victims to burn centers at Birmingham, AL; Louisville, KY; Cincinnati, OH, and Durham NC.

These missions led to two important developments in aeromedical evacuation procedures. First, the possibility of other disasters like the one at Waverly spurred efforts to help civilian organizations speed their requests for USAF air evacuation response. Second, the USAF

Directorate of Transportation provided the commanders of the 375th's four aeromedical evacuation squadrons with a list of burn care centers in the United States. The American Burn Association approved the list.

15 APRIL 1978: In response to a botulism epidemic in Clovis, NM, the severity of the disease, and the resulting lack of space at civilian hospitals in Clovis, a C-9A airlifted 11 victims of the virus from Clovis to medical facilities in Albuquerque. According to the Communicable Disease Center in Atlanta, GA, the epidemic was the second largest outbreak of the disease since health officials had begun tracking cases of botulism in 1899. The C-9A's quick response to the botulism outbreak in Clovis was credited with helping avert a civil disaster of major proportions.

27 MARCH 1979: A C-9A, S/N 71-10875, from the 9th Aeromedical Evacuation Squadron, Clark AB, PI,

flew the first C-9A mission to the People's Republic of China (PRC), landing at the Hung Chiao Airport, Shanghai. The crew gave the attending physician, Dr. E. V. Wong, and his staff from the PRC a tour of the C-9A before transporting two patients to the USAF hospital at Clark AB.

25 MAY 1979: Members of the Italian folk dancing group "Group Folkloristico Angelica" were injured in a bus accident in Greece. Because of the close relationship between the civilian community and Aviano AB, the Mayor of Aviano requested assistance from COL James W. Dearborn, commander at Aviano AB, Italy. A C-9A aircrew from the 435th Tactical Airlift Wing and a medical crew from the 2nd Aeromedical Evacuation Squadron, Rhein-Main AB, Germany, flew 18 injured members home to Aviano, Italy.

26 JUNE 1979: CAPT Christine E. Schott qualified as a C-9A aircraft commander, the first woman to do so in the 375th Aeromedical Airlift Wing.

19-20 NOVEMBER 1979: On 4 November, about 500 Iranian militants seized the US embassy in Iran and took about 90 hostages, including some 65 Americans. The 375th Aeromedical Airlift Wing C-9As airlifted the 3 Americans released on 19 November and the 10 released on 20 November.

25 APRIL 1980: Five servicemen who had been injured in an aborted rescue attempt for the hostages in Iran were flown by C-9A from the

Middle East to Ramstein AB, Germany. The rescue mission was called off due to equipment failure, but 8 Americans were killed and 5 were injured during the pullout in a collision between a CH-53 and a C-130.

8 JUNE 1980: A C-9A flown by MAC's first all-female aircrew launched from Scott AFB, IL. The crewmembers were: CAPT Susan R. Regele, CAPT Christine E. Schott, CAPT Catherine D. Young, CAPT Patricia A. Boland, SSgt Michele L. Varney, SrA Linda M. Sappington, SrA Marilyn C. Bates and A1C Genita E. Martino.

12 JULY 1980: The 375th AAW airlifted one of the 53 American hostages held in Iran since the takeover of the US embassy in November 1979. The hostage, released because of deteriorating health, was initially flown to Zurich, Switzerland, for medical treat-

Above, Capt. Christine E. Schott of the 11th AAS was the first woman in the 375th AAW to become an aircraft commander. (USAF) Bottom, MAC C-9A, S/N 71-0958, from the 375th AAW at Kelly AFB on 21 November 1982. (Phillip Friddell)

ment, but on the same day, he was transferred by C-9A to the Wiesbaden Regional Medical Center, West Germany.

20 JANUARY 1981: Two C-9As, bedecked with yellow ribbons, assigned to the 435th Tactical Airlift Wing and accompanied by medical crews from the 2nd Aeromedical Evacuation Squadron at Rhein-Main AB, Germany, flew to Algiers, Algeria. There, the C-9As picked up the 52 former hostages who had been released by Iran after 444 days of captivity. The two aircraft airlifted the

released Americans to Rhein-Main. Each C-9A carried 26 former hostages, 11 crewmembers, and 9 State Department representatives.

The two C-9As landed at Rhein-Main at 0444 local time, where the freed Americans were greeted by a large crowd of their fellow countrymen and more than 1,500 media representatives from 253 international news organizations. On 20 January, former Secretaries of States Cyrus R. Vance and Edmund S. Muskie flew from Washington, DC, to West Germany to greet the former hostages. Former President Jimmy Carter followed the next day and informed the former hostages of the many diplomatic efforts to secure their release. Both parties traveled on C-137s and on Sunday, 25 January, one of the C-137s brought the 52 Americans home.

MARCH 1981: Headquarters MAC and the 375th AAW Surgeon released a policy ordering each C-9A

medical crew to advise all personnel aboard each aeromedical evacuation flight that smoking should be kept to a minimum. They would also briefly explain why there was not smoking section available on aeromedical evacuation flights.

2 SEPTEMBER 1981: MAJ Jack W. Jones, Chief, Aeromedical Evacuation Division, Office of the MAC Surgeon, suggested that all of the C-9As in the Air Force should be equipped with an inertial navigation system package. In 1981, C-9As were not equipped with enhanced navigational aids, and, when operating over large expanses of water, navigation errors sometimes occurred.

2 DECEMBER 1981: MAC's Directorate of Maintenance

Above, C-9A, S/N 71-0880, one of two 435th TAW Nightingales that airlifted 52 American hostages freed by Iran to Rhein-Main AB, Germany, on 20 January 1981. (USAF) Bottom, the 435th's two C-9As devoid of any US markings at Rhein-Main prior to their flight to Algiers where they picked up the 52 former hostages who had been released after 444 days. (USAF)

Engineering notified the 374th TAW that inertial navigation system (INS) capability would be provided for the three C-9As at Clark AB, PI. With INS, the C-9As would be able to serve the greater Western Pacific theater, circumvent severe weather conditions, and use less fuel than the C-141s. C-141s were flying routes that could have been covered more eco-

nomically by C-9s equipped with an INS package. Previously, C-9As had to fly indirect routes in order to utilize external navigational aids.

25 JUNE 1982: A C-9A flew to Senegal, Africa, to provide aeromedical evacuation support for the NASA space shuttle mission. A Medical Service Corps officer and an anesthesiologist from the Weisbaden Hospital in Germany augmented the basic medical crew.

17 SEPTEMBER 1982: A commercial DC-10 passenger aircraft crashed in Malaga, Spain. Passengers suffered first and second-degree burns as well as smoke inhalation. A C-141 transported the patients to McGuire AFB, NJ, where some of the patients were carried aboard a waiting C-9A aircraft, which transported them to Boston, MA, and Buffalo, NY.

22 APRIL 1983: A C-9A airlifted two individuals injured in the bombing of the Beirut Embassy in Lebanon on 18 April. The C-9A flew the patients to Rhein-Main AB, Germany, after

which the injured were taken by ambulance to the nearby Wiesbaden Regional Medical Center, before continuing to the Continental United States.

23 OCTOBER THROUGH 9 DECEMBER 1983: Within three hours of notification of the bombing of the Marine barracks in Beirut, Lebanon, a C-9A remaining overnight at Adana, Turkey, diverted to Beirut and airlifted the first group of injured Marines to Rhein-Main AB, Germany.The bombing killed 241 Marines. The C-9A was assigned to the 435th TAW. The 375th AAW medical crew came from the 2nd Aeromedical Evacuation Squadron, which, like the 435th, was stationed at Rhein-Main AB, Germany. In all, 78 patients were airlifted on 7 missions, 5 C-9 and 2 C-141 missions.

25 OCTOBER THROUGH 19 NOVEMBER 1983: During Operation Urgent Fury, 375th AAW C-9As flew 32 patients on 6 missions. After Grenada experienced a leftist takeover, President Ronald Reagan ordered an invasion to protect United

Above, MAC C-9A, S/N 68-8935, from the 375th AAW at Buckley AFB in 1984. (Mike Wilson collection) Bottom, MAC C-9A, S/N 68-8932, from the 375th AAW at Laughlin, AZ, on 22 March 1986. By this time, United States Air Force was painted midway on the upper fuselage, replacing U.S. Air Force on the nose of the fuselage. (Phillip Friddell)

States interests as well as stability in the Caribbean. The operation provided a rare opportunity for assessing the interface of tactical and domestic aeromedical evacuations with combat forces in action.

25-29 APRIL 1984: The 375th AAW's 9th Aeromedical Evacuation Squadron from Clark AB, PI, supported President Ronald Reagan's trip to China with a dedicated C-9A and a crew on 24-hour alert status.

11 JUNE 1984: The first C-9A to receive the new paint scheme arrived at Scott AFB, IL, after programmed depot maintenance. Also, the "U.S. Air Force" markings were removed

and replaced with "United States Air Force".

19 JULY 1985: GEN Thomas M. Ryan, Jr., MAC Commander in Chief, and BGEN Veron Chong, Command Surgeon, proposed a no-smoking policy aboard all aeromedical evacuation C-9A missions. The ban applied to all passengers, patients, attendants, and crewmembers.

DECEMBER 1985: GEN Duane H. Cassidy, Commander in Chief of the MAC, and senior US military leaders in Europe agreed to incorporate continental United States C-9A aircraft into the European war plans. C-9As would move patients between third and fourth-echelon medical care facilities in a relatively low-threat environment of rear areas, away from combat zones. They would not operate into austere airfields or on roughened runways that contained minimal repairs after experiencing an airfield attack.

7 NOVEMBER 1986: In Project Hope, the 31st Aeromedical Evacuation Squadron and the 300th MAC Reserve Squadron at Charleston AFB joined the 375th AAW on a mission sponsored jointly by the US State and Defense Departments to airlift 15 children from earthquake-stricken San Salvador. A 375th AAW C-9A transported 12 of the children from Andrews AFB, MD, to a Shriners Hospital in Boston, MA.

MAY 1987: A missile attack from an Iraqi warplane killed 36 US Navy crewmembers aboard the USS Stark as it maneuvered in the Persian Gulf. Along with a C-141, a C-9A transported injured personnel to medical facilities in the United States.

23 SEPTEMBER 1987: For the first time, a Scott AFB C-9A deployed to West Germany as a part of the annual REFORGER (Return of Forces to Germany) exercise. This was a major strategic exercise to demonstrate America's commitments to the North Atlantic Treaty Organization (NATO)

Above, MAC C-9A, S/N 71-0877, from the 375th AAW at Randolph AFB on 20 May 1989. (Phillip Friddell) Bottom, MAC C-9A, S/N 67-22584, from the 375th AAW at Randolph AFB on 17 May 1991. (Phillip Friddell)

in wartime or crisis situations that involved the army and air forces of the United States, Great Britain, and Germany. The C-9's successful mission involved transporting simulated battle casualties and other patients from Germany to Great Britain.

9 FEBRUARY 1989: A C-141 assigned to the 437th MAW, Charleston AFB, SC, brought 37 Armenian children and young adults seriously injured in a 7 December 1988 earthquake from Rhein-Main AB, Germany, to Andrews AFB, MD. The children had been taken to Rhein-Main from Moscow and Yerevan several days before. A 375th AAW C-9A airlifted 12 children and their escorts from Andrews AFB, MD, to hospitals in Buffalo and Syracuse, NY, for gratuitous medical treatment.

22 DECEMBER 1989 THROUGH 14 FEBRUARY 1990: During Operation Just Cause, the contingency to oust military dictator GEN Manuel Noriega who was aligned with the drug trade and to restore democracy in Panama, C-9A missions were flown daily from San Antonio, TX, to 16 destinations throughout the United States. In all, the C-9As transported 256 military

Above, MAC C-9A, S/N 71-0874, in flight. (USAF) Bottom, MAC C-9A, S/N 68-8934, at Fighter Town USA, NAS Miramar, CA, in May 1989. (Ginter)

patients to their home units for further medical treatment of convalescent leave.

21 JUNE 1990: A C-9A from the 375th MAW at Scott AFB airlifted seven burn patients to Brooke Army Medical Center, TX. The victims suffered burns from a fire on the USS Midway.

27 FEBRUARY 1991: C-9As deployed to Myrtle Beach AFB, SC, to await orders to support Operation Desert Shield and Operation Desert Storm during the Persian Gulf War. Patients returning stateside were fewer than anticipated, so the C-9As were not needed.

16 OCTOBER 1993: The "City of Belleville", a C-9 belonging to the 375th AAW at Scott AFB, transported a US Army pilot, CWO3 Michael Durant, from Andrews AFB, MD, to Fort Campbell, KY, his home station. Injured following the downing of his helicopter and 11 days of captivity in Somalia, Durant had been medevaced on non-AMC aircraft from Mogadishu , Somalia, to the Army Regional Medical Center at Landstuhl, Germany, on 15 October. A C-141 medevac flight next took him from Ramstein AB, Germany, to Andrews. A medical crew from the 57th Aeromedical Evacuation Squadron, Scott AFB, cared for Durant on the mission from Andrews to Fort Campbell. While onboard the aircraft, Durant was awarded the Purple Heart and the Armed Forces Expeditionary Medal.

21 OCTOBER 1993: NASA requested C-9A support to transport 4 shuttle astronauts and 28 mission support personnel from Edwards AFB, California, to Ellington Field in Houston, TX. NASA medical teams wanted to conduct evaluations on the crew immediately after a mission to determine the effects of space flight. This required the shuttle crew to be transported lying prone.

23 MARCH 1994: An F-16D Fighting Falcon collided with a C-130 Hercules transport while both were attempting to land at Pope AFB, NC. The explosion and resulting fire killed 23 Army paratroopers and severely injured 83 others who had been training nearby. One C-9A diverted from Raleigh-Durham, NC, to Fayetteville, NC. A second C-9A flew from Scott AFB. Both aircrews reconfigured the

Above, dual use 375th AAW/932nd AAW (reserve) C-9A, S/N 71-0958, at Edwards AFB. (Ginter) Bottom, MAC 375th AAW C-9A, S/N 68-8932, in flight. (Harry Gann)

adcraft to carry eight-litter tiers before transporting 20 severely burned victims to Kelly AFB, TX, for specialized treatment at the Army Burn Center at nearby Fort Sam Houston. Debris from the F-16 fell on a parked C-141 and on Army forces waiting to board the Starlifter for an airborne training exercise. The resulting fire killed at least 20 and destroyed the C-141.

5 OCTOBER 1994: A C-9A aircrew, assisted by an 11-person neonatal team from Wilford Hall Medical Center in San Antonio, TX, transported a 19-day-old infant from Omaha, NE, to Scott AFB, IL, for heart transplant surgery at Children's Hospital in St. Louis. US Senator Robert Kerrey

(NE Democrat) requested the medevac mission. A C-9A crew on a routine mission to Kelly AFB, TX, was tasked en route to pick up the team at Wilford Hall and take it to Omaha. Because of the long crew day, a second C-9A launched from Scott AFB to bring the baby and medical team to southern Illinois from Nebraska.

14 JULY 1995: Members of the 11th Airlift Squadron and the 375th Aeromedical Evacuation Squadron transported members of the Space Shuttle Atlantis in a C-9A from Kennedy Space Center in FL to Ellington Field in Houston, TX. The shuttle members, returning from the Russian Mir Space Station, included two Russian cosmonauts and one American astronaut.

29 JUNE 1996: Rodeo is the Air Mobility Command-sponsored biennial event which tests the flying and support skills of competing aircrews, combat controllers, aerial porters, security police, and maintainers. Beginning with Rodeo 96, held between 21 and 28 June at McChord AFB, WA, aeromedical evacuation crews, like C-17 crews, participated for the first time. Twenty-two aeromedical evacuation teams used three types of aircraft; Four of those teams used the C-9A. The 375th Aeromedical Evacuation Squadron won "Best C-9A Crew".

22 OCTOBER 1996: In a goodwill effort, a C-9A responded to a cargo aircraft crash in Manta, Ecuador. At least 20 people were killed and 60 seriously injured. The C-9A flew to Kelly AFB, TX, to pick up doctors, nurses, and medical technicians. Upon arrival, the teams treated victims in the coastal areas of Manta, Portoviejo, and Guayaquil.

27 NOVEMBER 1996: A 375th AAW C-9A crew picked up an 11-member neo-natal intensive care unit from Wilford Hall Medical Center, Lakeland AFB, TX. It then flew them to Winston-Salem, NC, to pick up a newborn infant girl with lung problems. The team used an inflight extra corporeal membrane oxygenation machine to allow the infant to bypass

her heart and lungs and transported her to the St. Louis Children's Hospital for further care.

22 APRIL 1997: President Bill Clinton toured flood-ravaged cities near Grand Forks AFB, ND, to assess damage and to commend community efforts. Nearly 60,000 residents were forced out of their homes when the Red River crashed through temporary clay levees and sandbag dikes. A C-9A and two Air National Guard helicopters air-evacuated some 45 critically ill patients to hospitals in the Minneapolis-St. Paul, MN, area.

9-23 JUNE 1997: For two weeks, the 932nd AAW (Reserve) and its 73rd Airlift Squadron, stationed at Scott AFB, took over full-time C-9A aeromedical evacuation missions from the 375th Airlift Wing at Scott AFB. This Phoenix Pace Program, implemented by GEN Ronald R. Fogleman on 1 January 1993 when he was commander of the AMC, gave the 932nd Airlift Wing a chance to train under full-time conditions and allowed the 375th to take care of personal and local training requirements.

7 AUGUST 1997: A 30th Airlift Squadron aircrew and its C-9A departed from Yokota AB, Japan, to deliver medical supplies to Anderson AFB, Guam. The supplies were for victims of the 6 August Korean Air jet-liner crash near Won Pat International Airport, Guam. Eight burn victims

from the crash of Korean Air Flight 801 returned home to South Korea aboard the C-9A.

APRIL 1998: Members of the 86th Aeromedical Evacuation Squadron from Ramstein AB, Germany, delivered the first baby in squadron history during a routine medical evacuation flight. The 75th Airlift Squadron C-9A aircraft and crew were flying pregnant women from Olbia, Sardinia, to Naples, Italy, when one woman went into labor. Edgar Phillip Santana was delivered in perfect health in only 38 minutes.

Below, the C-9A as they appeared after 15 October 1999. The United States of America replaced United States Air Force on the upper fuselage side and the red cross on the tail was removed. (USAF)

21 JUNE 1998: For the second consecutive Rodeo competition, the 375th Aeromedical Evacuation Squadron won the trophy for best C-9A team.

13 AUGUST 1998: After 12 Americans perished in a terrorist bombing of the US embassy in Nairobi, Kenya, on 7 August, a C-17 assigned to the 437th AAW, Charleston AFB, SC, returned the remains of 10 American victims to Andrews AFB, MD. On 12 August, a C-5 from the 436th AAW, Dover AFB, DE, returned the body of an eleventh victim, SMSgt Sherry Lynn Olds, from Ramstein AB, Germany, to Dover. A C-9A assigned to the 375th AAW, Scott AFB, took Sgt Olds' remains from Dover to Tyndall AFB, FL, for internment at her hometown, Panama City, at her family's request. The twelfth American victim, married to a Kenyan, was buried in Kenya.

26 AUGUST 1998: A C-9A crew departed Scott AFB to evacuate patients from Langley AFB, VA, to Andrews AFB, MD, before Hurricane Bonnie struck the East Coast. All patients moved required altitude restriction, intravenous fluids, oxygen, and cardiac monitoring.

17 MARCH 1999: Poland, the Czech Republic, and Hungary held ceremonies marking the accession of the former Warsaw Pact countries into the North Atlantic Treaty Organization. Allied Air Forces Central Europe Commander GEN John P. Jumper, accompanied by an entourage of about 20 North Atlantic Treaty Organization military officials, traveled aboard a C-9A to attend the ceremonies.

29 APRIL THROUGH 29 JULY 1999: The 375th AAW at Scott AFB deployed its C-9A named "City of Mascoutah" to Ramstein AB, Germany, to help handle US casualties that came out of Kosovo. Approximately 20 personnel deployed, half active duty and half

Above, C-9A, S/N 71-0880, in Germany in 2002. (Harry Gann) Bottom, C-9A sistership, S/N 71-0879, in Germany in 2002. (Harry Gann)

from its Air Force Reserve affiliate, the 932nd AW also at Scott. During its stay at Ramstein, the aircraft and crew were attached to the USAF in Europe, augmenting the five C-9As stationed there. According to COL Bradley S. Baker, the 375th AW commander, "This is the first time we've done this since we got the C-9As here" in August 1968. The airplane and crews returned to Scott on 29 July 1999.

2 MAY 1999: A C-9A transported three former Army prisoners of war, SPC Steven Gonzales and SSgts Christopher Stone and Andrew Ramirez, to Ramstein AB, Germany, from Zagreb, Croatia. They had been captured by Serbian forces while patrolling in the former Yugoslav

Republic of Macedonia during Operation Allied Force. Members of the 86th Aeromedical Evacuation Squadron, who flew aboard the mission, assisted the men.

4 JUNE 1999: A C-9A from Scott AFB flew an urgent aeromedical evacuation mission to Haiti to bring eight critically injured sailors back to the US following a truck accident. The mission earned the crew Wing Aircrew of the Quarter as well as the 1999 Fifteenth Air Force Aircrew Excellence Award presented during the Fifteenth Air Force Commanders' Conference at the annual Solano Trophy banquet at Travis AFB, CA.

16-30 JULY 1999: C-9As from Scott AFB teamed up with aeromedical specialists in the US Navy and member nations of NATO for Joint Task Force Exercise 99-2 in the Atlantic. The joint-service training exercise was needed to support the Aerospace Expeditionary Force concept.

15 OCTOBER 1999: The C-9A program manager, Don Beyer, 375th Logistics Support Squadron, announced that the Air Force's entire fleet of C-9As would e given a new external appearance. The new outward look, which required repainting, removed the designation United States Air Force, replaced it with United States of America, and eliminated the traditional Air Force 'star and bars" logo. The aircraft's traditional white, gray, and black colors remained. In 1999, C-9As were

assigned not only to the AMC but also to the USAF in Europe and the Pacific Air Forces. The aircraft of all three major commands were painted differently. C-9As had previously been repainted when permanently reassigned among the three commands. The new, standardized pattern of external design eliminated the requirement for repainting to match other aircraft in theater. The C-9As would be repainted during programmed depot maintenance at the aircraft's primary contractor, Lockheed-Martin, Greenville, SC. Every C-9A underwent large-scale depot maintenance every five years. Repainting was a 10-day-long process.

5 MAY 2000: A 375th AAW C-9A transported members of the 375th AES and the 932nd AES from Scott AFB to participate in Rodeo 2000 at Pope AFB, NC. More than 100 teams from the active duty Air Force, Air Force Reserve Command, and Air National Guard, as well as allied nations, compete in the biennial event in areas such as airdrop, air refueling, aeromedical evacuation, security forces, and short-field landings. For Rodeo 2000, a new event was added to the aeromedical evacuation competition. The Aeromedical Evacuation Obstacle Course required the team to transport one casualty by litter through various obstacles using proper body mechanics and proper lifting techniques. This event was added in addition to C-9A pre-flight, configuration, enplaning, aeromedical emergency scenarios, and medical equip-

ment pre-flight and operation. The aeromedical evacuation team from Scott placed second.

21 OCTOBER 2000: On 12 October, the explosion of a bomb-laden terrorist boat tore a large gash on the port side of the USS Cole as it was anchored in the port of Aden, Yemen. The explosion occurred on the destroyer's port side near the main dining area killing 17 sailors and wounding 39. On 21 October, a 375th AAW C-9A transported one of the injured survivors on the final leg of her journey from Andrews AFB, MD, to NAS Norfolk, VA.

12 FEBRUARY 2001: The Air Force directed the removal of the Red Cross emblem from the C-9A fleet so the aircraft could be used for missions other than aeromedical airlift. International law, as prescribed under the Geneva Convention, restricts using C-9As marked with the red cross to medical missions. Units operating C-9As were given until January 2002 to complete removing the red cross markings in the most efficient and cost-effective manner. The area of the tail where the Red Cross had been displayed would be left void of markings to allow the emblem to be reapplied in the event of a military contingency or a wartime operation.

Below, 75th AS/86th AW C-9A, S/N 71-0882, in 2003. (Mark Aldrich collection)

USAF C-9A COCKPIT, S/N 71-0958, 1997

Ginter

USN / USMC C-9B COCKPIT

Harry Gann

FLIGHT COMPARTMENT SEATS

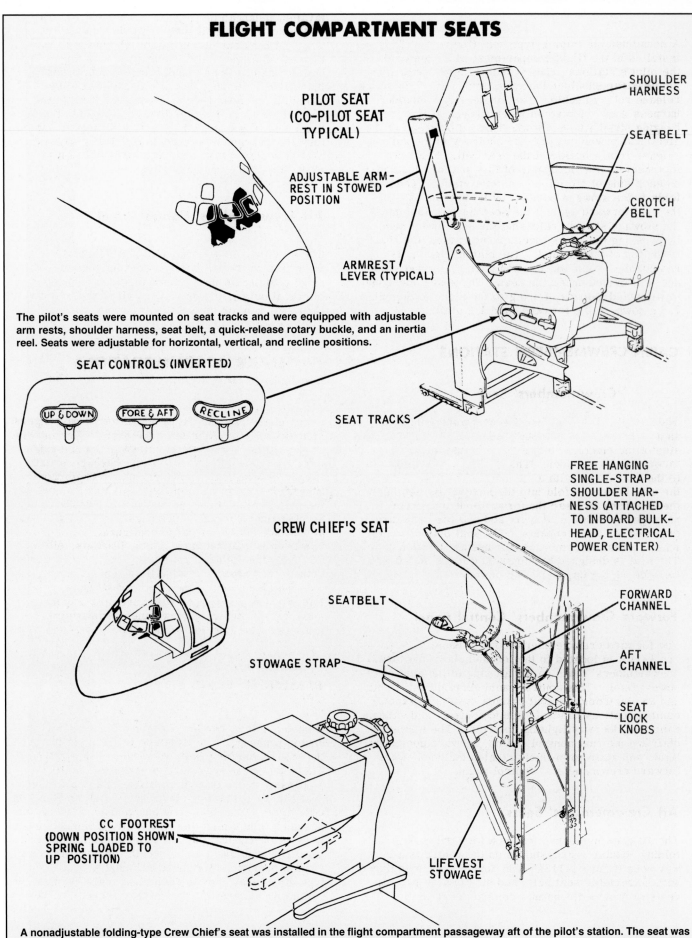

PILOT SEAT (CO-PILOT SEAT TYPICAL)

SHOULDER HARNESS

SEATBELT

CROTCH BELT

ADJUSTABLE ARM-REST IN STOWED POSITION

ARMREST LEVER (TYPICAL)

The pilot's seats were mounted on seat tracks and were equipped with adjustable arm rests, shoulder harness, seat belt, a quick-release rotary buckle, and an inertia reel. Seats were adjustable for horizontal, vertical, and recline positions.

SEAT CONTROLS (INVERTED)

UP & DOWN   FORE & AFT   RECLINE

SEAT TRACKS

CREW CHIEF'S SEAT

FREE HANGING SINGLE-STRAP SHOULDER HAR-NESS (ATTACHED TO INBOARD BULK-HEAD, ELECTRICAL POWER CENTER)

SEATBELT

FORWARD CHANNEL

AFT CHANNEL

STOWAGE STRAP

SEAT LOCK KNOBS

CC FOOTREST (DOWN POSITION SHOWN, SPRING LOADED TO UP POSITION)

LIFEVEST STOWAGE

A nonadjustable folding-type Crew Chief's seat was installed in the flight compartment passageway aft of the pilot's station. The seat was equipped with a single-strap shoulder harness, seat belt, and a quick-release rotary buckle. Folddown footrests were located on each side of the pilot's center console. The seat folds against the left side of the cockpit entry wall for stowage.

USAF C-9A BUILT - IN STRETCHER LOADING RAMP

The main cargo door (81 inches by 136 inches) was located on the left side of the fuselage aft of the forward passenger door. The door was manually controlled and hydraulically operated by pressure from the right hydraulic system. The hand pump in the right hand main gear well could be used to supply hydraulic pressure for operating the door if normal hydraulic system pressure was not available. The cargo door was hinged at the top and opened upward and outward. Latches located along the lower edge of the door locked the door in the closed position. The door could be locked open in either the 84° or 162° position.

In the USAF C-9As, a built-in stretcher loading walk-up ramp was included. What follows are nine photos of this ramp being deployed. (all photos Harry Gann)

USAF C-9A CABIN AND TYPICAL INTERIOR ARRANGEMENTS

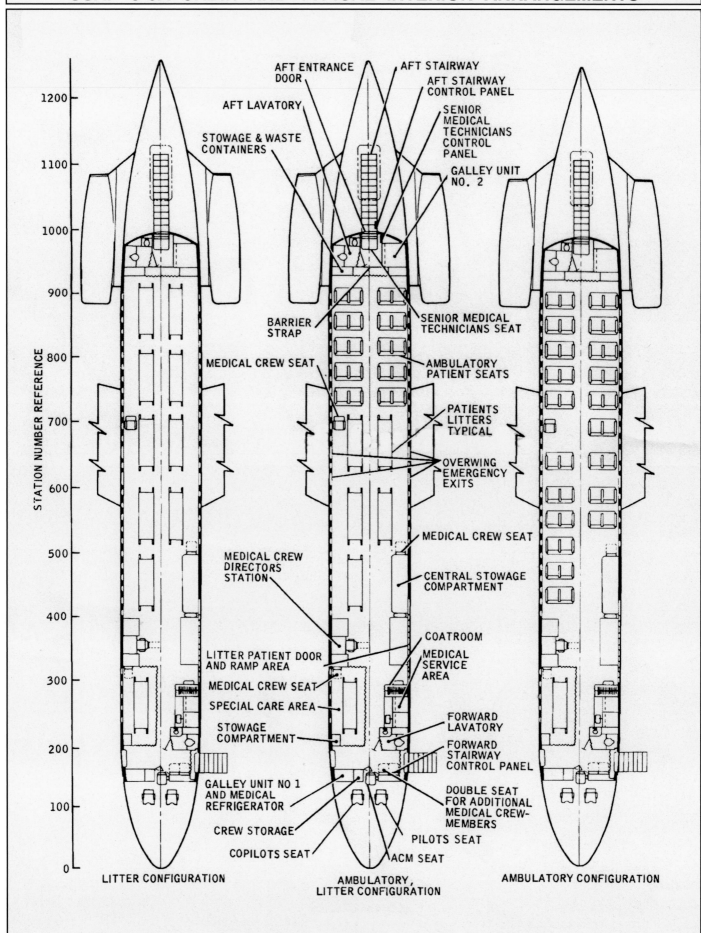

AFT ENTRANCE DOOR
AFT STAIRWAY
AFT STAIRWAY CONTROL PANEL
AFT LAVATORY
SENIOR MEDICAL TECHNICIANS CONTROL PANEL
STOWAGE & WASTE CONTAINERS
GALLEY UNIT NO. 2
BARRIER STRAP
SENIOR MEDICAL TECHNICIANS SEAT
MEDICAL CREW SEAT
AMBULATORY PATIENT SEATS
PATIENTS LITTERS TYPICAL
OVERWING EMERGENCY EXITS
MEDICAL CREW SEAT
CENTRAL STOWAGE COMPARTMENT
MEDICAL CREW DIRECTORS STATION
COATROOM
MEDICAL SERVICE AREA
LITTER PATIENT DOOR AND RAMP AREA
MEDICAL CREW SEAT
SPECIAL CARE AREA
FORWARD LAVATORY
STOWAGE COMPARTMENT
FORWARD STAIRWAY CONTROL PANEL
GALLEY UNIT NO 1 AND MEDICAL REFRIGERATOR
DOUBLE SEAT FOR ADDITIONAL MEDICAL CREW-MEMBERS
CREW STORAGE
PILOTS SEAT
COPILOTS SEAT
ACM SEAT

STATION NUMBER REFERENCE

1200
1100
1000
900
800
700
600
500
400
300
200
100
0

LITTER CONFIGURATION

AMBULATORY, LITTER CONFIGURATION

AMBULATORY CONFIGURATION

22

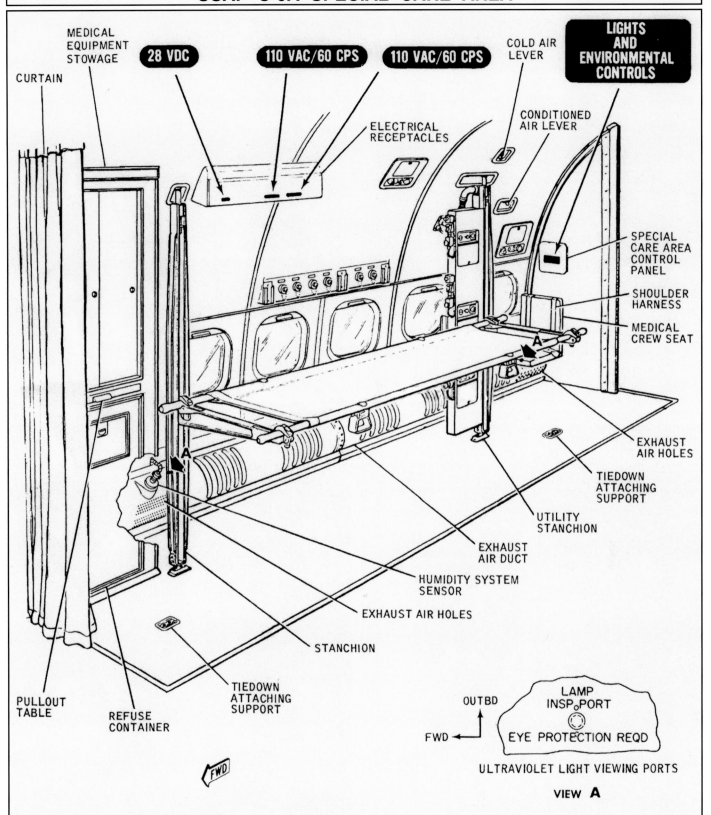

28 VDC

110 VAC/60 CPS

110 VAC/60 CPS

LIGHTS AND ENVIRONMENTAL CONTROLS

MEDICAL EQUIPMENT STOWAGE

CURTAIN

ELECTRICAL RECEPTACLES

COLD AIR LEVER

CONDITIONED AIR LEVER

SPECIAL CARE AREA CONTROL PANEL

SHOULDER HARNESS

MEDICAL CREW SEAT

EXHAUST AIR HOLES

TIEDOWN ATTACHING SUPPORT

UTILITY STANCHION

EXHAUST AIR DUCT

HUMIDITY SYSTEM SENSOR

EXHAUST AIR HOLES

STANCHION

TIEDOWN ATTACHING SUPPORT

PULLOUT TABLE

REFUSE CONTAINER

FWD

A

A

OUTBD

FWD

LAMP INSP PORT

EYE PROTECTION REQD

ULTRAVIOLET LIGHT VIEWING PORTS

VIEW **A**

The special care area was located in the cabin just forward of the nurses station. The area, when in use, was enclosed by a manual draw curtain supported at the ceiling on a track. The area was separately ventilated and incorporated a device at the lower edge of the curtain to maintain a taut surface and minimize air leakage. Accommodations for four litter patients were provided with access to the patient's head, foot, and sides. Three consoles were provided on the utility stanchion and one in the upper sidewall. A single forward facing folding seat was located at the aft end of the special care area for a medical crewmember. This crewmember was provided with a console containing the same utilities as the patients and was located on the cabin wall above the seat. The call switch on the console was for requesting assistance from another medical crewmember. A stowage compartment for medical supplies was located at the forward end of this area. A pullout table and a metal refuse container was installed in the stowage compartment below the equipment stowage space.

USAF C-9A MEDICAL SERVICE AREA

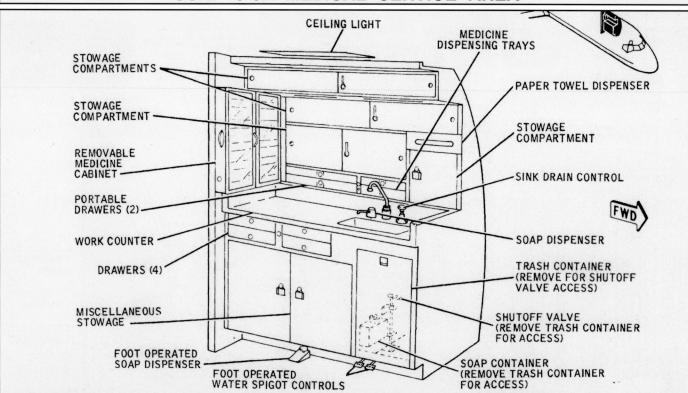

CEILING LIGHT

MEDICINE DISPENSING TRAYS

STOWAGE COMPARTMENTS

STOWAGE COMPARTMENT

REMOVABLE MEDICINE CABINET

PORTABLE DRAWERS (2)

WORK COUNTER

DRAWERS (4)

MISCELLANEOUS STOWAGE

FOOT OPERATED SOAP DISPENSER

FOOT OPERATED WATER SPIGOT CONTROLS

PAPER TOWEL DISPENSER

STOWAGE COMPARTMENT

SINK DRAIN CONTROL

FWD

SOAP DISPENSER

TRASH CONTAINER (REMOVE FOR SHUTOFF VALVE ACCESS)

SHUTOFF VALVE (REMOVE TRASH CONTAINER FOR ACCESS)

SOAP CONTAINER (REMOVE TRASH CONTAINER FOR ACCESS)

The medical service area was located on the forward left side of the cabin directly across from the special care area. A stainless steel sink was installed with a work counter, drain control knob, liquid-soap dispenser, and medical type faucet. Stowage and trash container compartments were installed below the sink. Above the stowage compartment were four drawers for medical supplies. A removable medicine cabinet with retaining racks was located on the left side. Two portable, partitioned drawers for medicine stowage were located directly above the work counter. Forward of these portable drawers were two special medicine dispensing trays. A stowage area was located above the medicine dispensing trays, and was accessible through sliding doors and used cushioned, separated holders.

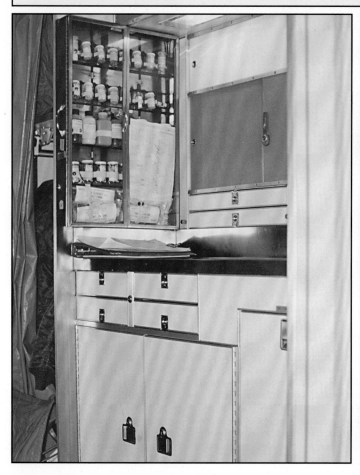

24

USAF C-9A NURSES STATION AND STORAGE

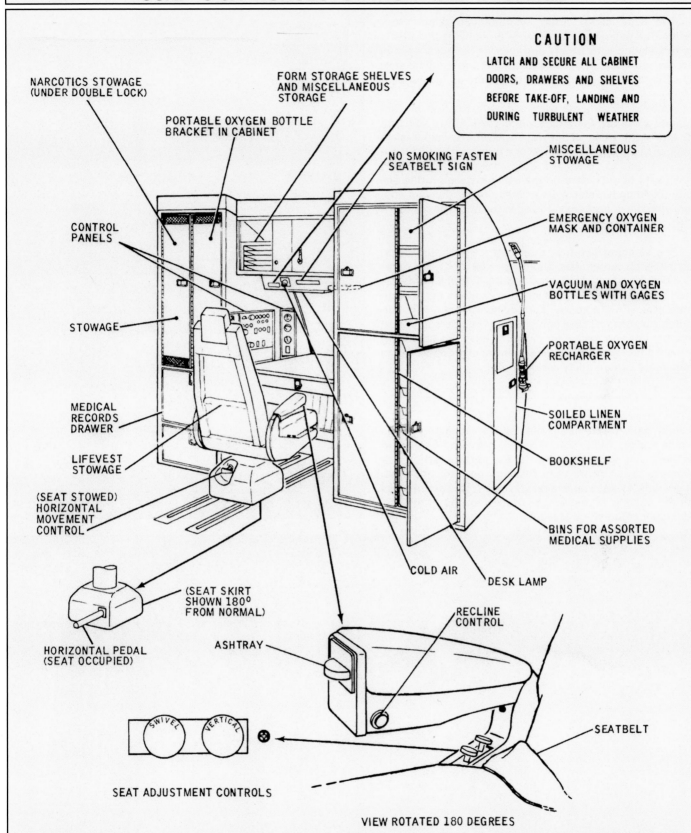

CAUTION
LATCH AND SECURE ALL CABINET DOORS, DRAWERS AND SHELVES BEFORE TAKE-OFF, LANDING AND DURING TURBULENT WEATHER

NARCOTICS STOWAGE (UNDER DOUBLE LOCK)

FORM STORAGE SHELVES AND MISCELLANEOUS STORAGE

PORTABLE OXYGEN BOTTLE BRACKET IN CABINET

NO SMOKING FASTEN SEATBELT SIGN

MISCELLANEOUS STOWAGE

CONTROL PANELS

EMERGENCY OXYGEN MASK AND CONTAINER

VACUUM AND OXYGEN BOTTLES WITH GAGES

STOWAGE

PORTABLE OXYGEN RECHARGER

MEDICAL RECORDS DRAWER

SOILED LINEN COMPARTMENT

LIFEVEST STOWAGE

BOOKSHELF

(SEAT STOWED) HORIZONTAL MOVEMENT CONTROL

BINS FOR ASSORTED MEDICAL SUPPLIES

COLD AIR

DESK LAMP

(SEAT SKIRT SHOWN 180° FROM NORMAL)

RECLINE CONTROL

HORIZONTAL PEDAL (SEAT OCCUPIED)

ASHTRAY

SEATBELT

SWIVEL   VERTICAL

SEAT ADJUSTMENT CONTROLS

VIEW ROTATED 180 DEGREES

The nurses station was located in the forward right portion of the cabin aft of the special care compartment. The station included a desk, chair, light, vacuum regulators and trap bottle assemblies, provisions for therapeutic oxygen assemblies, cold air outlet, emergency oxygen and mask container, cabinets, control panels, and circuit breakers. Slanted shelves above the desk were provided for blank forms and were covered by sliding doors. A lockable metal narcotics compartment behind a lockable cabinet door was located adjacent to and forward of the desk. The seat was equipped with a seat belt and was mounted on tracks to allow positioning from the centerline of the aircraft to the stored position against the desk. The seat had to face aft during takeoff and landing. The seat could also be raised, lowered, or reclined. All seat adjustments were controlled by a simple lever accessible to the seat occupant.

USAF C-9A CABIN UTILIZATION

The C-9A cabin could accommodate ambulatory and/or litter patients. Other interior furnishings included a nurse's station with supply and records cabinets, special care compartment, medical sink and pharmaceutical supply storage, an aft galley, and forward and aft lavatories.

Ambulatory patients were accommodated in aft facing, first-class style airliner seats in rows of two seats on left and right sides of the fuselage with a center aisle between them. Spacing allows for a maximum of 40 ambulatory patients to be carried. Seat track and litter support attachment fittings were permanently installed in the aircraft. Rapid conversion from ambulatory to litter was possible with the seats being stowed in the baggage compartment.

The standard two-row, three-high litter configuration had a 27-inch center aisle. There was a 66-inch head clearance between the outside litter and the sidewall of the aircraft. This arrangement provided for 27 litters in the main cabin plus 3 in the special care compartment. Air conditioning, oxygen, reading lights, and a nurse's call button were provided for each litter patient in the utility stanchion of each litter tier. Utility tiers were easily converted to ambulatory patient utility racks.

At right, early C-9As had laminated wood cabinets at the nurses station. (Harry Gann) Below, later built C-9As had synthetic plastic coated cabinets. The nurse's station was located in the forward right fuselage opposite the main cargo door. All passenger seats faced aft. This aircraft was configured with 30 passenger seats and one litter rack. (Air Mobility Command Museum)

Above, C-9A configured with 40-seats for ambulatory patients looking forward towards the cockpit. (Air Mobility Command Museum) Below, C-9A configured for 30-seats. (Harry Gann)

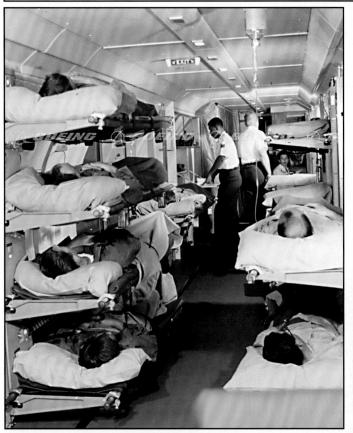

Above left, C-9A configured 100% with litters. Above right, mix of litter and ambulatory patients looking forward. Bottom, two litters in the first tier aft of the nurse's station. (all photos Harry Gann)

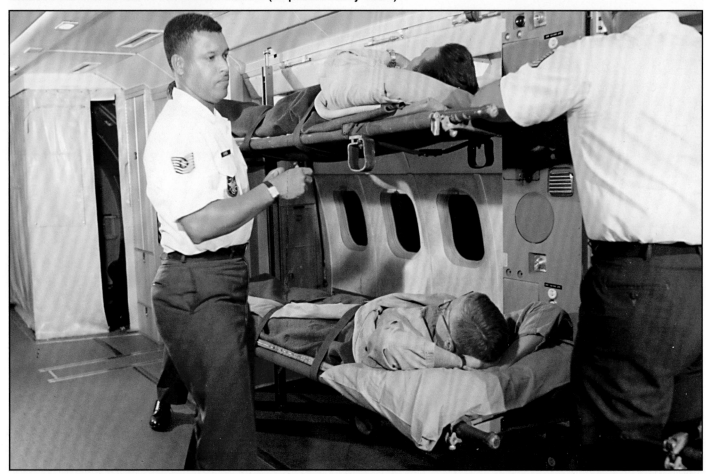

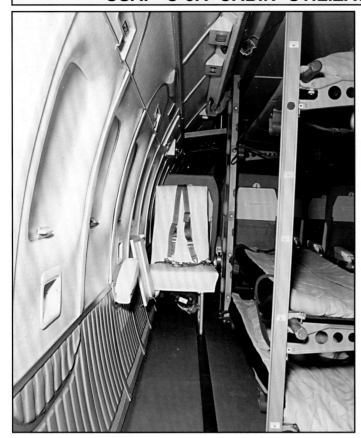 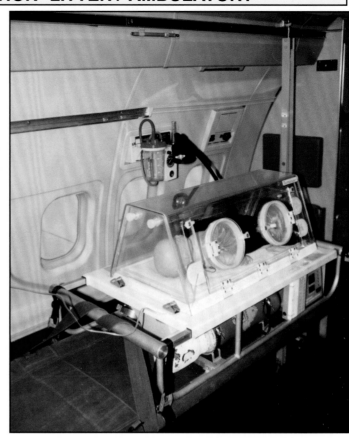

Above left, both sides of the litter tiers were accessable for patient care. Note right overwing seat installed between the fuselage and the litter tiers. (Harry Gann) Above right, incubator installation. (Ginter) Below, cargo includes gurney. (Ginter)

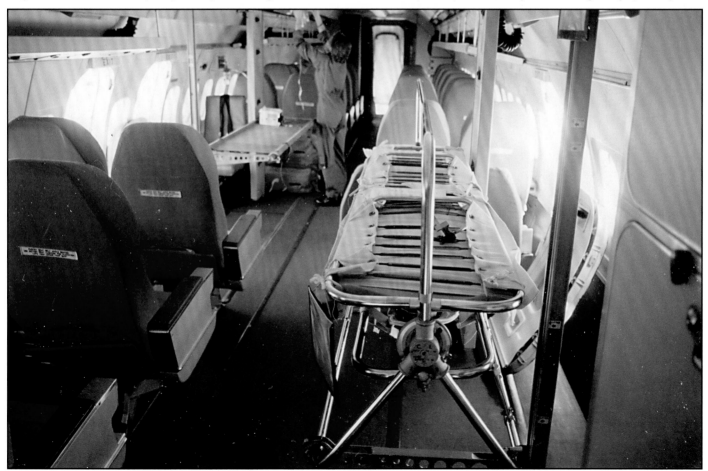

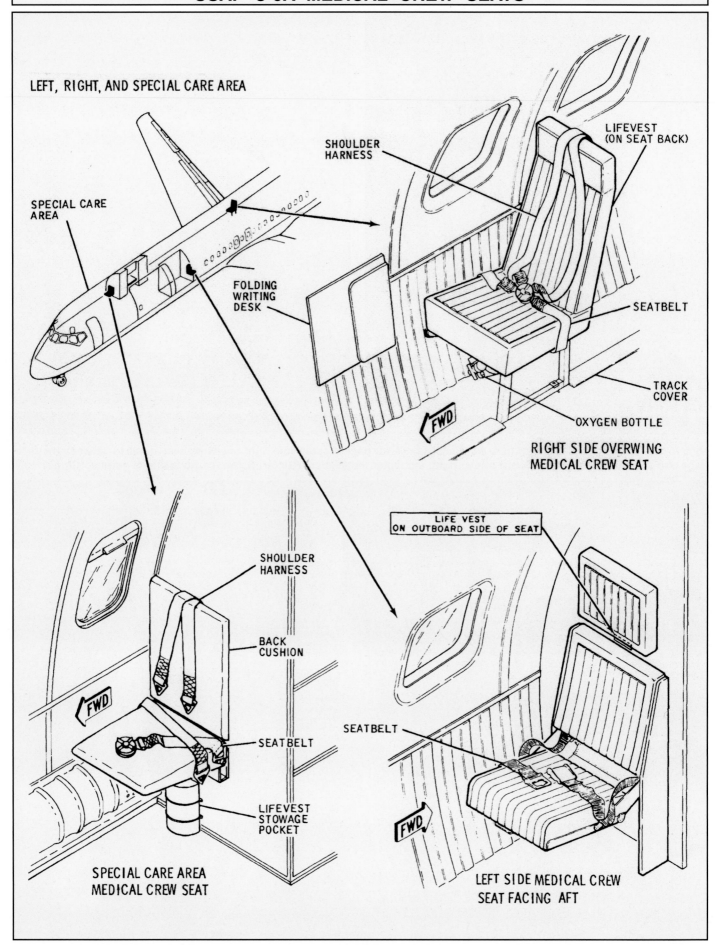

LEFT, RIGHT, AND SPECIAL CARE AREA

SPECIAL CARE AREA

SHOULDER HARNESS

LIFEVEST (ON SEAT BACK)

FOLDING WRITING DESK

SEATBELT

TRACK COVER

OXYGEN BOTTLE

FWD

RIGHT SIDE OVERWING MEDICAL CREW SEAT

SHOULDER HARNESS

BACK CUSHION

SEATBELT

LIFEVEST STOWAGE POCKET

FWD

SPECIAL CARE AREA MEDICAL CREW SEAT

LIFE VEST ON OUTBOARD SIDE OF SEAT

SEATBELT

FWD

LEFT SIDE MEDICAL CREW SEAT FACING AFT

C-9 EMERGENCY EXITS

Three inflatable, fire-resistant evacuation slides were installed, one each in the forward entrance door, the forward service door, and at the aft end of the walkway in the tail section. Six emergency escape ropes were installed, one over each pilot's window and one over each overwing emergency exit.

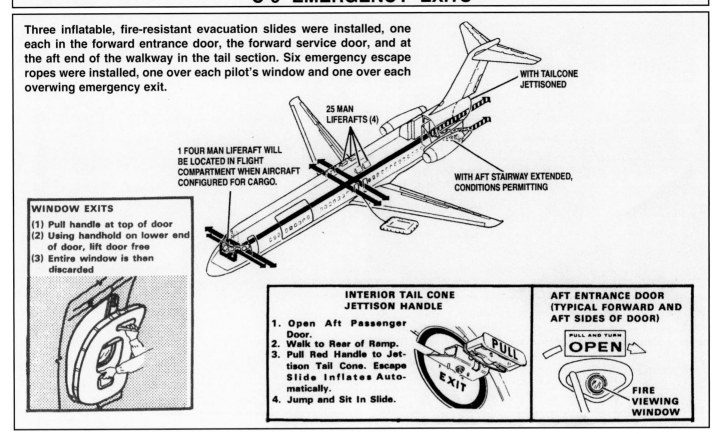

WITH TAILCONE JETTISONED

25 MAN LIFERAFTS (4)

1 FOUR MAN LIFERAFT WILL BE LOCATED IN FLIGHT COMPARTMENT WHEN AIRCRAFT CONFIGURED FOR CARGO.

WITH AFT STAIRWAY EXTENDED, CONDITIONS PERMITTING

WINDOW EXITS
(1) Pull handle at top of door
(2) Using handhold on lower end of door, lift door free
(3) Entire window is then discarded

INTERIOR TAIL CONE JETTISON HANDLE
1. Open Aft Passenger Door.
2. Walk to Rear of Ramp.
3. Pull Red Handle to Jettison Tail Cone. Escape Slide Inflates Automatically.
4. Jump and Sit In Slide.

PULL EXIT

AFT ENTRANCE DOOR (TYPICAL FORWARD AND AFT SIDES OF DOOR)
PULL AND TURN
OPEN
FIRE VIEWING WINDOW

USAF C-9A AFT GALLEY

The after galley on the C-9A contained a cold water tap that provided chilled drinking water and a sink that incorporated hot and cold water faucets. A thermostatically controlled electrical water heater was located within the galley. Water was drained into an overboard drain mast. Forty-eight compact, stowage-type serving trays were also provided.

The electrical refrigerator was divided into two compartments with separate doors. The freezer compartment provided space for stowage for 48 frozen meals, 2 ice cube trays, and other miscellaneous articles. Temperature was maintained at or below 0° F by a preset thermostat and was not adjustable by the flight crew. The freezer had an ON/OFF toggle switch with an indicator light when the unit was operating. The cooler compartment provided space for items requiring chilling. Temperature was maintained at 40° F. In addition to the freezer/cooler compartments, a separate ice cube stowage drawer was installed.

The oven was divided into two separate, stainless steel heating compartments, containing racks that were easily removed from the galley. Each oven compartment had an independent temperature control with an ON/OFF switch and incorporated a 0-to-60 minute timer with a buzzer that sounded when the timing cycle was complete.

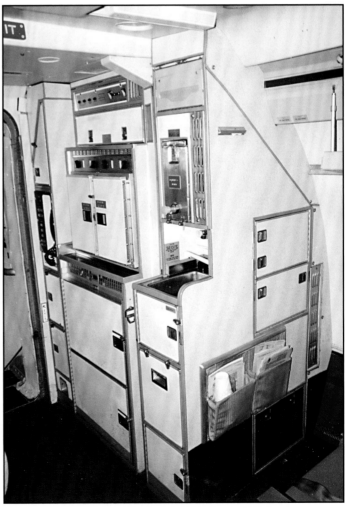

At right, the aft galley configuration on the USAF C-9A was located in the left aft fuselage adjacent to the tail mounted aft fuselage door. (Ginter)

C-9 EMERGENCY OXYGEN SYSTEM

C-9A CENTRAL STORAGE COMPART.

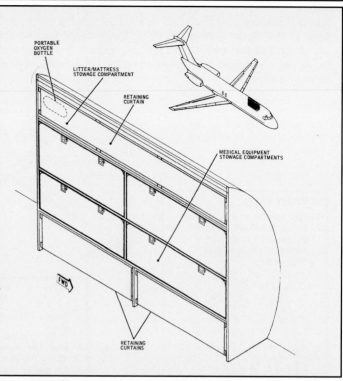

PORTABLE
OXYGEN
BOTTLE

LITTER/MATTRESS
STOWAGE COMPARTMENT

RETAINING
CURTAIN

MEDICAL EQUIPMENT
STOWAGE COMPARTMENTS

FWD

RETAINING
CURTAINS

Above, C-9 emergency oxygen panel was above each passenger row. (Harry Gann) Bottom left, included in the C-9A forward galley was a medical refrigerator (note compressor screen) for drugs, vaccines and solutions seen here at bottom right. (Harry Gann) Later aircraft had aftermarket off-the-shelf refrigerators as seen at bottom right. (Ginter)

USAF C-9A FRONT GALLEY EARLY

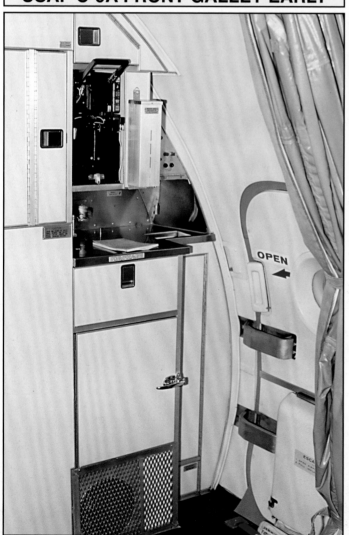

USAF C-9A FRONT GALLEY LATE

USN / USMC C-9B FRONT AND AFT GALLEYS

Two galley units were installed in the C-9B cabin. Galley One was located forward of the right forward service/emergency exit door. It contained an oven, coffee makers, electrical control panel, and stowage space. The inboard surface contained Omega access and C.P.I. battery stowage.

Galley Two was located in the aft section on the left side of the aircraft opposite the aft lavatory and adjacent to the aft passenger door. It contained an electric control panel, a work counter with light, oven coffee maker, freezer, portable emergency light, miscellaneous galley equipment, and the aft flight attendant's control panel.

A 30-gallon pressurized, potable water tank supplies water to galleys. Waste water from both galleys was drained into a removable container within the galleys. All drawers, doors, and bins incorporated latches to prevent accidental or inadvertent opening.

At left, C-9B forward galley. (Harry Gann)

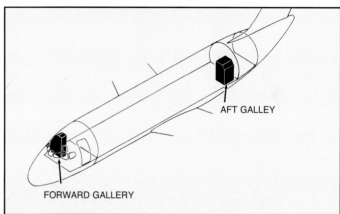

AFT GALLEY

FORWARD GALLERY

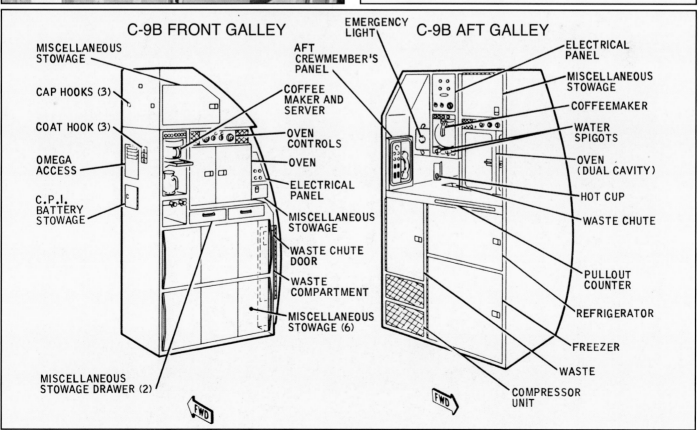

C-9B FRONT GALLEY

MISCELLANEOUS STOWAGE

CAP HOOKS (3)

COAT HOOK (3)

OMEGA ACCESS

C.P.I. BATTERY STOWAGE

MISCELLANEOUS STOWAGE DRAWER (2)

EMERGENCY LIGHT

AFT CREWMEMBER'S PANEL

COFFEE MAKER AND SERVER

OVEN CONTROLS

OVEN

ELECTRICAL PANEL

MISCELLANEOUS STOWAGE

WASTE CHUTE DOOR

WASTE COMPARTMENT

MISCELLANEOUS STOWAGE (6)

C-9B AFT GALLEY

ELECTRICAL PANEL

MISCELLANEOUS STOWAGE

COFFEEMAKER

WATER SPIGOTS

OVEN (DUAL CAVITY)

HOT CUP

WASTE CHUTE

PULLOUT COUNTER

REFRIGERATOR

FREEZER

WASTE

COMPRESSOR UNIT

FWD

FWD

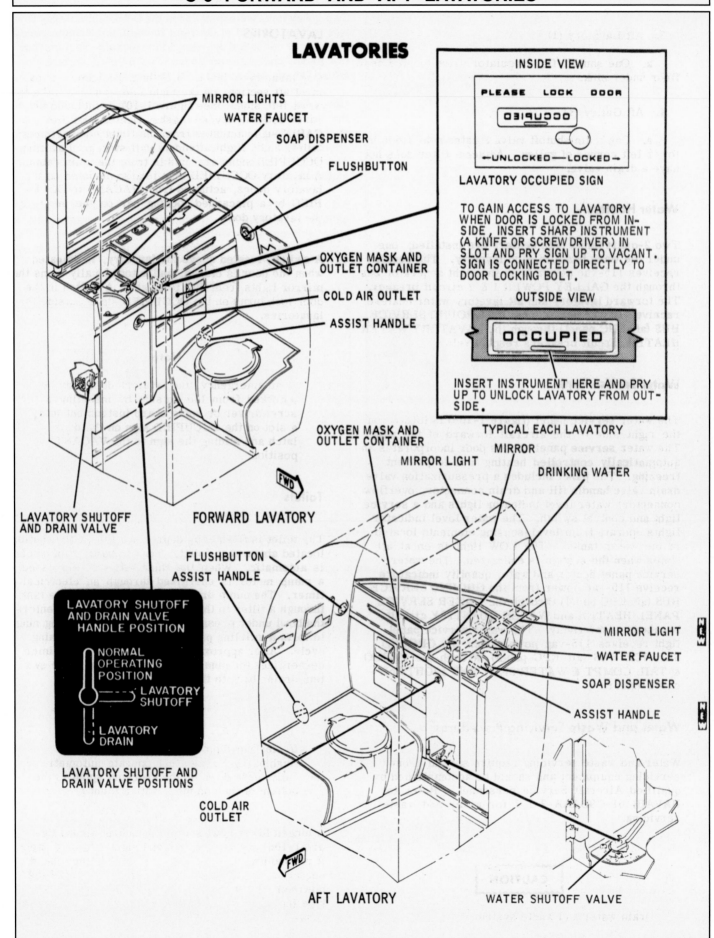

LAVATORIES

MIRROR LIGHTS
WATER FAUCET
SOAP DISPENSER
FLUSHBUTTON

OXYGEN MASK AND
OUTLET CONTAINER
COLD AIR OUTLET
ASSIST HANDLE

LAVATORY SHUTOFF
AND DRAIN VALVE

FORWARD LAVATORY

INSIDE VIEW

PLEASE LOCK DOOR

OCCUPIED

—UNLOCKED — LOCKED—

LAVATORY OCCUPIED SIGN

TO GAIN ACCESS TO LAVATORY
WHEN DOOR IS LOCKED FROM IN-
SIDE, INSERT SHARP INSTRUMENT
(A KNIFE OR SCREW DRIVER) IN
SLOT AND PRY SIGN UP TO VACANT.
SIGN IS CONNECTED DIRECTLY TO
DOOR LOCKING BOLT.

OUTSIDE VIEW

OCCUPIED

INSERT INSTRUMENT HERE AND PRY
UP TO UNLOCK LAVATORY FROM OUT-
SIDE.

TYPICAL EACH LAVATORY

OXYGEN MASK AND
OUTLET CONTAINER
MIRROR
MIRROR LIGHT
DRINKING WATER

FLUSHBUTTON
ASSIST HANDLE

LAVATORY SHUTOFF
AND DRAIN VALVE
HANDLE POSITION

NORMAL
OPERATING
POSITION
LAVATORY
SHUTOFF
LAVATORY
DRAIN

LAVATORY SHUTOFF AND
DRAIN VALVE POSITIONS

MIRROR LIGHT
WATER FAUCET
SOAP DISPENSER
ASSIST HANDLE

COLD AIR
OUTLET

AFT LAVATORY

WATER SHUTOFF VALVE

PASSENGER SEATS

The C-9B maximum passenger capacity was 90, but in an emergency 107 could be carried by reducing the seat pitch from 38° to 34° and removing the coat rooms. Unlike in the USAF C-9A, the C-9B seats were mounted facing forward. Stowage space was provided for luggage in the forward and aft lower baggage compartments (433 cu.ft.) and in the cabin overhead storage racks. Additional space was available in the forward-left cabin for small items, and two removable coat racks were located in the aft cabin.

Seats, upholstered in flame-resistant fabrics, provided a high level of comfort. All armrests, except those adjacent to the emergency exit aisle, folded flush with the seat back, and a folding service tray was installed on the back of each seat.

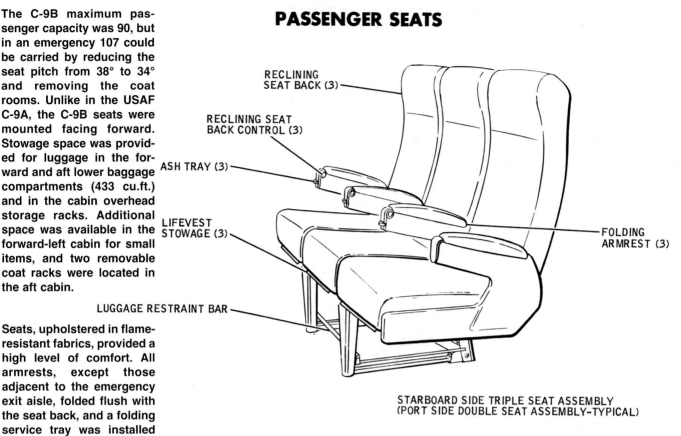

STARBOARD SIDE TRIPLE SEAT ASSEMBLY
(PORT SIDE DOUBLE SEAT ASSEMBLY–TYPICAL)

PRINCIPAL DIMENSIONS
INTERIOR

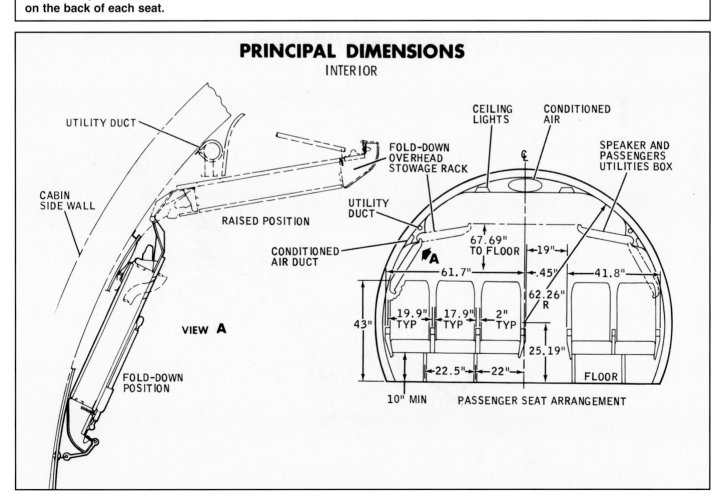

VIEW A

PASSENGER SEAT ARRANGEMENT

USN / USMC C-9B 90 PASSENGERS GENERAL ARRANGEMENT

Accommodations were provided for 90 passengers in addition to the flight crew members. The interior configuration was easily convertible to accommodate full cargo or any combination of passengers and cargo. Seating arrangements for passenger configurations were in rows of five seats across, two on the port side and three on the starboard side. Sectionalized stowage racks capable of being folded down for cargo configurations were provided for stowage of hats, coats, blankets, pillows, etc. Reading lights, cold air outlets, oxygen mask outlets, and crew member call switches were provided in the bottom of the overhead stowage racks. Each window was equipped with vertically moving shades and acoustic window panes installed integrally with the interior window trim panels.

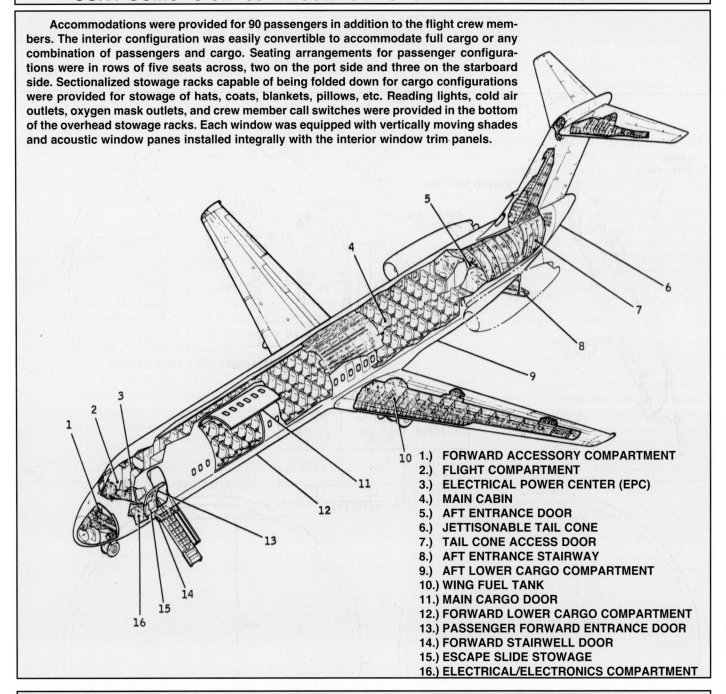

1.) FORWARD ACCESSORY COMPARTMENT
2.) FLIGHT COMPARTMENT
3.) ELECTRICAL POWER CENTER (EPC)
4.) MAIN CABIN
5.) AFT ENTRANCE DOOR
6.) JETTISONABLE TAIL CONE
7.) TAIL CONE ACCESS DOOR
8.) AFT ENTRANCE STAIRWAY
9.) AFT LOWER CARGO COMPARTMENT
10.) WING FUEL TANK
11.) MAIN CARGO DOOR
12.) FORWARD LOWER CARGO COMPARTMENT
13.) PASSENGER FORWARD ENTRANCE DOOR
14.) FORWARD STAIRWELL DOOR
15.) ESCAPE SLIDE STOWAGE
16.) ELECTRICAL/ELECTRONICS COMPARTMENT

USN / USMC C-9B 45 PASSENGERS AND 3 LARGE PALLETS

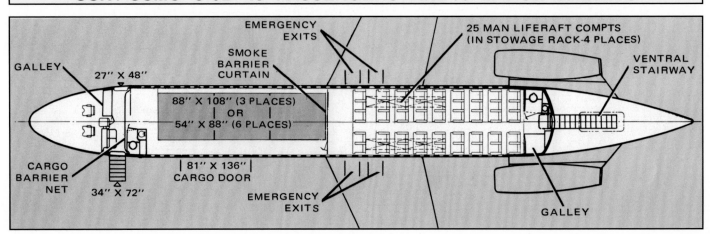

USN / USMC C-9B 65 SEATS AND 2 LARGE CARGO PALLETS

USN / USMC C-9B 7 SEATS AND 7 LARGE CARGO PALLETS

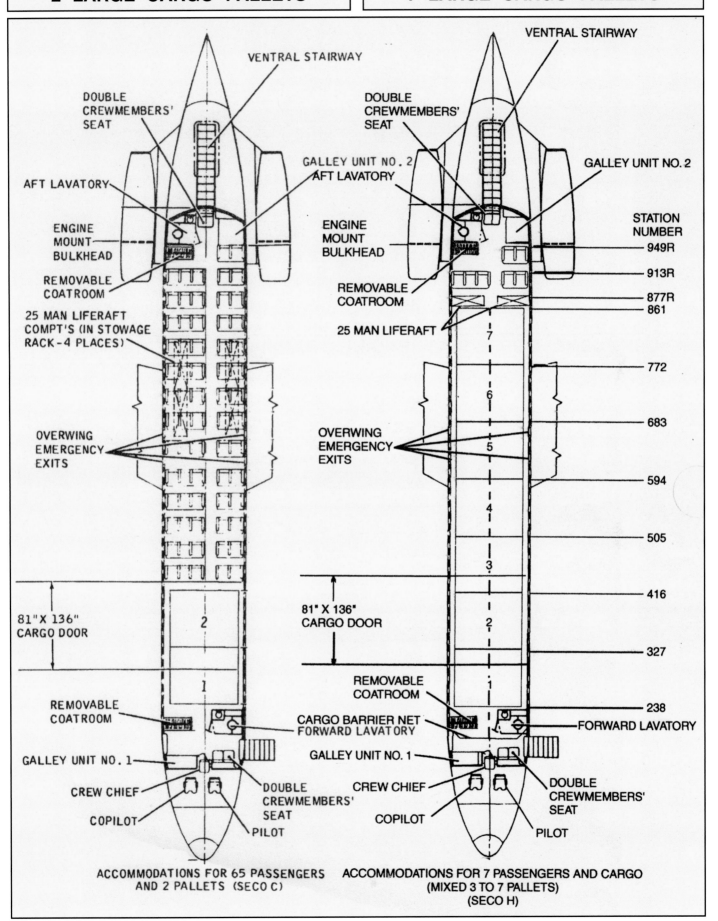

Left diagram labels:

- VENTRAL STAIRWAY
- DOUBLE CREWMEMBERS' SEAT
- AFT LAVATORY
- GALLEY UNIT NO. 2
- ENGINE MOUNT BULKHEAD
- REMOVABLE COATROOM
- 25 MAN LIFERAFT COMPT'S (IN STOWAGE RACK – 4 PLACES)
- OVERWING EMERGENCY EXITS
- 81" X 136" CARGO DOOR
- REMOVABLE COATROOM
- GALLEY UNIT NO. 1
- CREW CHIEF
- COPILOT
- DOUBLE CREWMEMBERS' SEAT
- PILOT

ACCOMMODATIONS FOR 65 PASSENGERS AND 2 PALLETS (SECO C)

Right diagram labels:

- VENTRAL STAIRWAY
- DOUBLE CREWMEMBERS' SEAT
- GALLEY UNIT NO. 2
- AFT LAVATORY
- ENGINE MOUNT BULKHEAD
- REMOVABLE COATROOM
- 25 MAN LIFERAFT
- OVERWING EMERGENCY EXITS
- 81" X 136" CARGO DOOR
- REMOVABLE COATROOM
- CARGO BARRIER NET FORWARD LAVATORY
- GALLEY UNIT NO. 1
- FORWARD LAVATORY
- CREW CHIEF
- DOUBLE CREWMEMBERS' SEAT
- COPILOT
- PILOT

STATION NUMBER
- 949R
- 913R
- 877R
- 861
- 772
- 683
- 594
- 505
- 416
- 327
- 238

ACCOMMODATIONS FOR 7 PASSENGERS AND CARGO (MIXED 3 TO 7 PALLETS) (SECO H)

USN / USMC C-9B INBOARD PROFILE PASSENGER CONFIGURATION

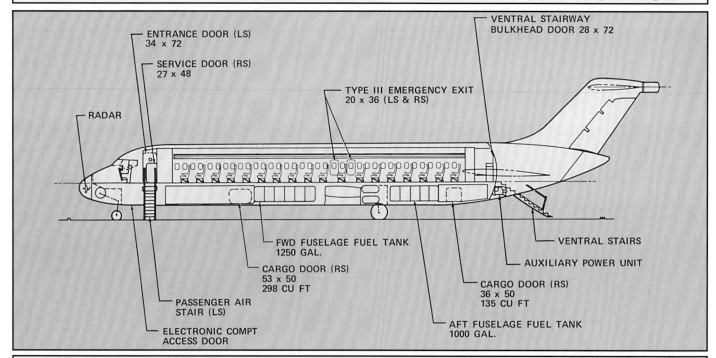

USN / USMC C-9B F-14A/B ENGINE TRANSPORT CONFIGURATION

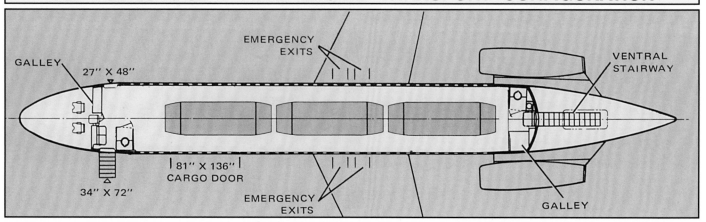

The C-9B could transport three containerized F-14A TF30-P412 engines or three F-14B N401-PW-400 engines or up to five non-containerized F-14A/B engines. The plan view illustrates how three conntainerized engines were loaded.

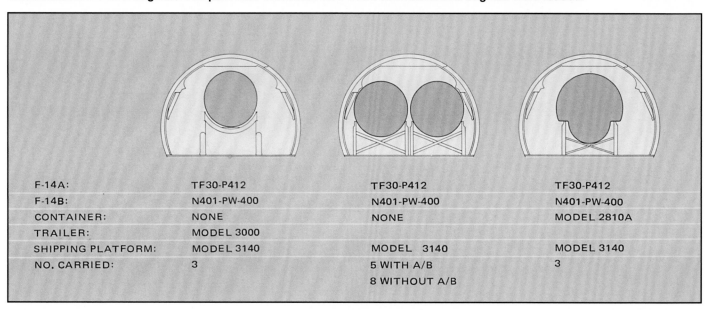

F-14A:	TF30-P412	TF30-P412	TF30-P412
F-14B:	N401-PW-400	N401-PW-400	N401-PW-400
CONTAINER:	NONE	NONE	MODEL 2810A
TRAILER:	MODEL 3000		
SHIPPING PLATFORM:	MODEL 3140	MODEL 3140	MODEL 3140
NO. CARRIED:	3	5 WITH A/B	3
		8 WITHOUT A/B	

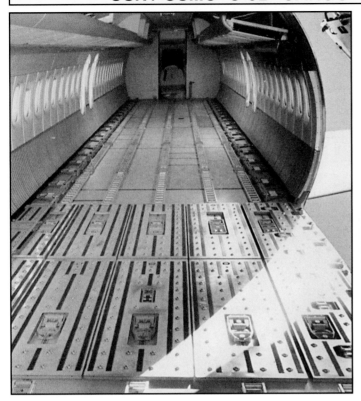

Above left, the cargo deck loading system was designed to accommodate military 463-L type pallets. Pallets were loaded through the main cargo door and placed on the ball transfer assemblies shown here. Above right, cargo pallets being loaded on a C-9B. Below, C-9B configured for 45 seats with three pallets loaded forward of the passengers. (all photos Harry Gann)

USN / USMC C-9B CARGO LOADING

Above, at Camp Darby on 18 Aug. 2008, Italian technicians working for the 405th Army Field Support Battalion assist VR-46 crew members in loading humanitarian supplies onto a C-9B Skytrain. The aircraft, based in Marietta, GA, represents the U.S. Navy's first asset participating in the ongoing humanitarian efforts in the Republic of Georgia. (USN)

USN / USMC C-9B CARGO LOADING VIA FORKLIFT

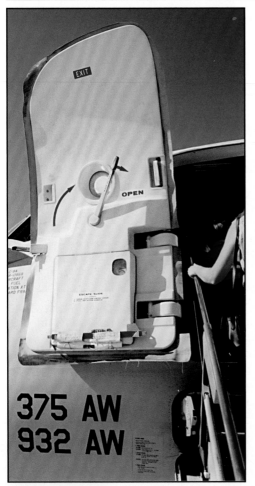

At left, forward passenger door open. Above, air-stairs for the forward entrance door deployed. Bottom, close-up of air-stair's hinge and stairwell hinge door in the open position. Note stairwell door release handle control recepticle well is open to the left. (all photos Ginter)

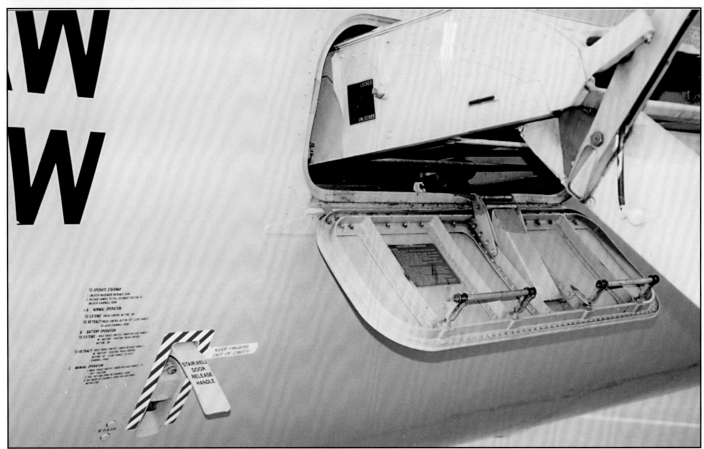

FORWARD ENTRANCE DOOR, SERVICE DOOR, AND STAIRWAY

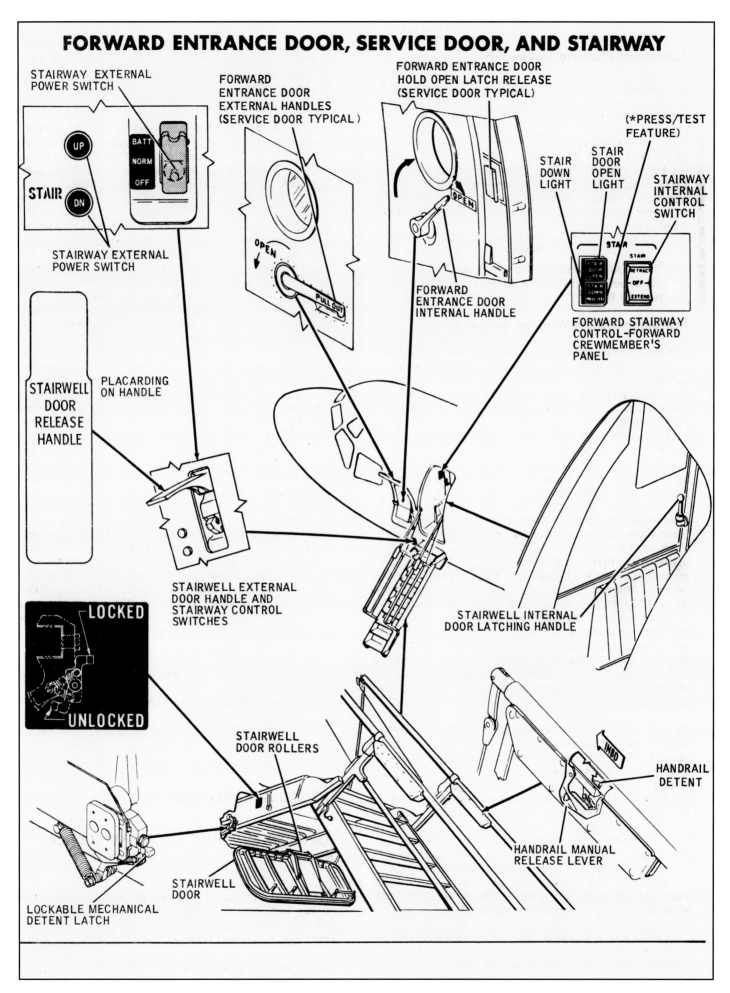

STAIRWAY EXTERNAL POWER SWITCH

STAIRWAY EXTERNAL POWER SWITCH

FORWARD ENTRANCE DOOR EXTERNAL HANDLES (SERVICE DOOR TYPICAL)

FORWARD ENTRANCE DOOR HOLD OPEN LATCH RELEASE (SERVICE DOOR TYPICAL)

(*PRESS/TEST FEATURE)

STAIR DOWN LIGHT

STAIR DOOR OPEN LIGHT

STAIRWAY INTERNAL CONTROL SWITCH

FORWARD ENTRANCE DOOR INTERNAL HANDLE

FORWARD STAIRWAY CONTROL-FORWARD CREWMEMBER'S PANEL

STAIRWELL DOOR RELEASE HANDLE

PLACARDING ON HANDLE

STAIRWELL EXTERNAL DOOR HANDLE AND STAIRWAY CONTROL SWITCHES

STAIRWELL INTERNAL DOOR LATCHING HANDLE

LOCKED

UNLOCKED

STAIRWELL DOOR ROLLERS

HANDRAIL DETENT

STAIRWELL DOOR

HANDRAIL MANUAL RELEASE LEVER

LOCKABLE MECHANICAL DETENT LATCH

C-9 AFT TAIL CONE ENTRANCE AND INTEGRAL AIR - STAIRS

The aft entrance door was mounted on the aft pressure bulkhead and hinged on the right side to swing forward against the lavatory wall. A viewing window was installed in the door handle recess to allow inspection of the stairway area with the door closed. The door provided access to the forward end of the aft stair passageway, where the interior aft entrance stairway control panel was located. The crew member's seat was attached to the door. The seat bottom was spring loaded and closed automatically into the door recess when not occupied. A barrier strap was installed across the aisle forward of the door for takeoff and landing. A two-position hold-open latch was installed on the right side of the aisle to hold the door in the open position. Door warning lights on the flight compartment annunciator panel remained on when the door was not closed and latched. (all photos Ginter)

AFT ENTRANCE DOOR AND STAIRWAY

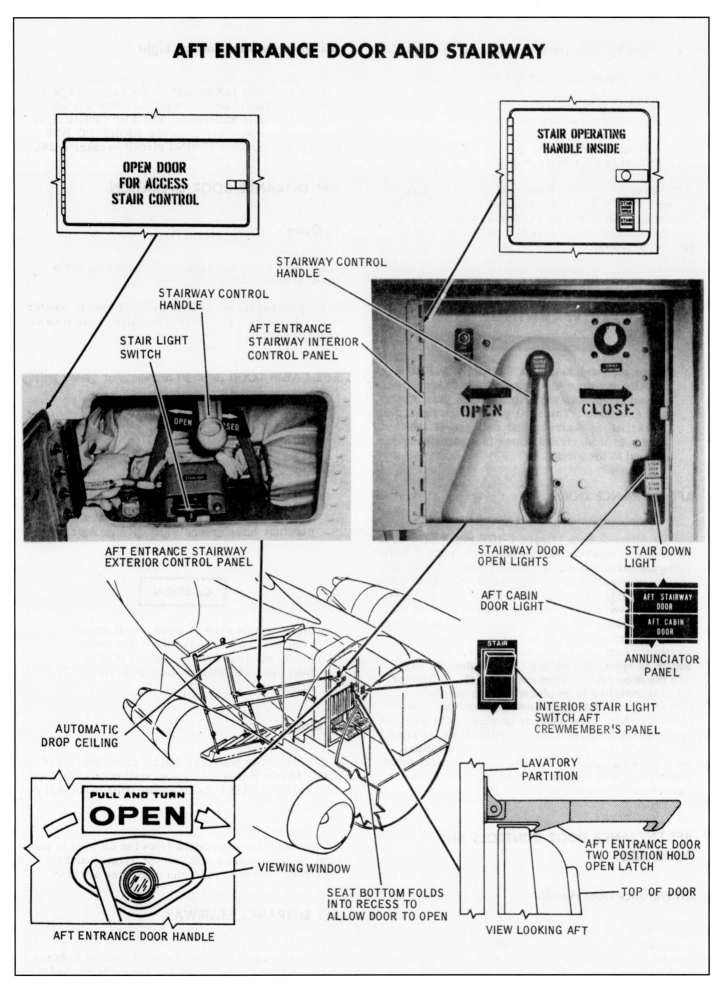

OPEN DOOR FOR ACCESS STAIR CONTROL

STAIR OPERATING HANDLE INSIDE

STAIR DOOR OPEN
STAIR DOWN

STAIRWAY CONTROL HANDLE

STAIRWAY CONTROL HANDLE

STAIR LIGHT SWITCH

AFT ENTRANCE STAIRWAY INTERIOR CONTROL PANEL

OPEN   CLOSE

STAIR DOOR OPEN
STAIR DOWN

AFT ENTRANCE STAIRWAY EXTERIOR CONTROL PANEL

STAIRWAY DOOR OPEN LIGHTS

STAIR DOWN LIGHT

AFT CABIN DOOR LIGHT

AFT STAIRWAY DOOR
AFT CABIN DOOR

ANNUNCIATOR PANEL

STAIR

INTERIOR STAIR LIGHT SWITCH AFT CREWMEMBER'S PANEL

AUTOMATIC DROP CEILING

PULL AND TURN OPEN

AFT ENTRANCE DOOR HANDLE

VIEWING WINDOW

SEAT BOTTOM FOLDS INTO RECESS TO ALLOW DOOR TO OPEN

LAVATORY PARTITION

AFT ENTRANCE DOOR TWO POSITION HOLD OPEN LATCH

TOP OF DOOR

VIEW LOOKING AFT

45

FORWARD AND AFT CABIN CREWMEMBER'S SEATS

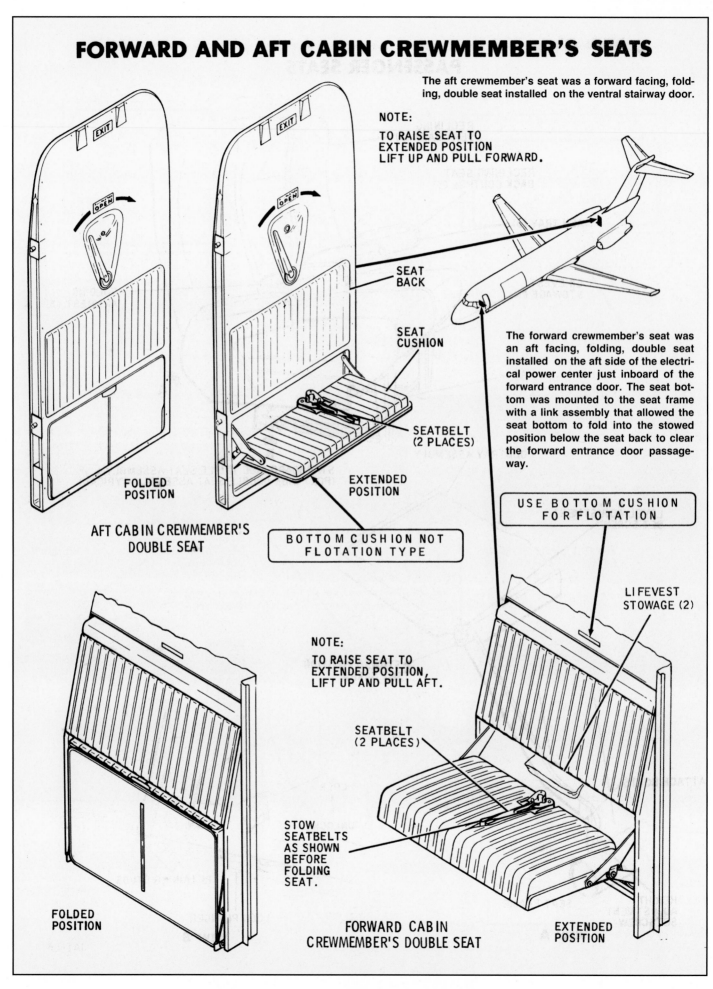

The aft crewmember's seat was a forward facing, folding, double seat installed on the ventral stairway door.

NOTE:

TO RAISE SEAT TO EXTENDED POSITION LIFT UP AND PULL FORWARD.

SEAT BACK

SEAT CUSHION

SEATBELT (2 PLACES)

FOLDED POSITION

EXTENDED POSITION

AFT CABIN CREWMEMBER'S DOUBLE SEAT

BOTTOM CUSHION NOT FLOTATION TYPE

The forward crewmember's seat was an aft facing, folding, double seat installed on the aft side of the electrical power center just inboard of the forward entrance door. The seat bottom was mounted to the seat frame with a link assembly that allowed the seat bottom to fold into the stowed position below the seat back to clear the forward entrance door passageway.

USE BOTTOM CUSHION FOR FLOTATION

LIFEVEST STOWAGE (2)

NOTE:

TO RAISE SEAT TO EXTENDED POSITION, LIFT UP AND PULL AFT.

SEATBELT (2 PLACES)

STOW SEATBELTS AS SHOWN BEFORE FOLDING SEAT.

FOLDED POSITION

FORWARD CABIN CREWMEMBER'S DOUBLE SEAT

EXTENDED POSITION

FORWARD AND AFT CREWMEMBER'S PANELS

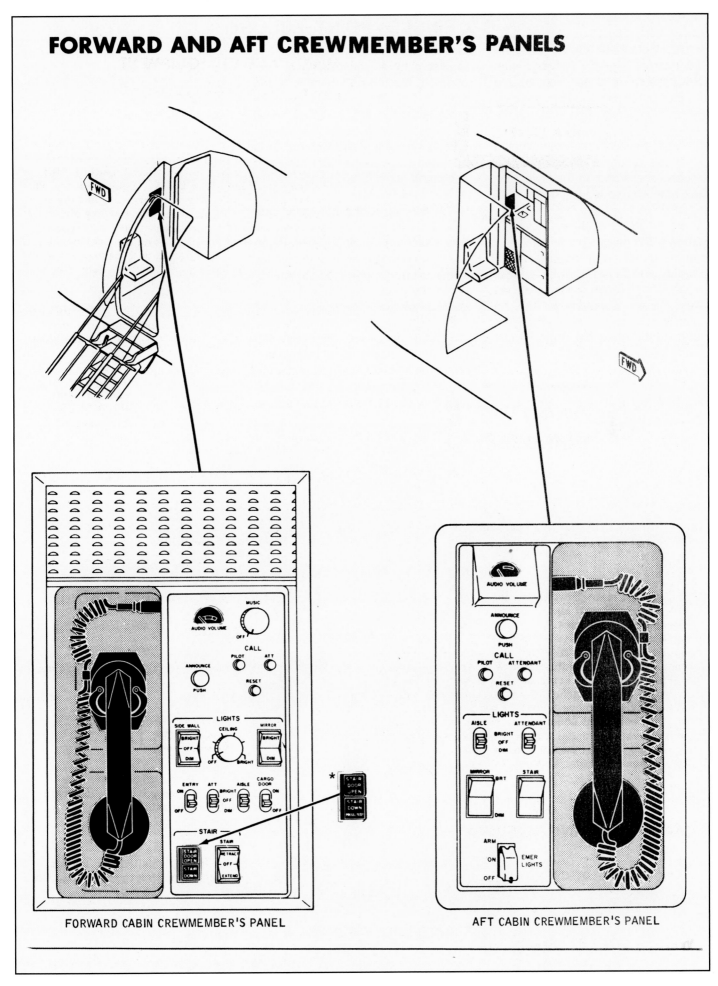

FORWARD CABIN CREWMEMBER'S PANEL

AFT CABIN CREWMEMBER'S PANEL

A single-point fueling adapter, with integral regulator (limiting manifold pressure to 50 psi), was located on the right-wing leading edge at approximately mid-span, and approximately 5.5 feet above ramp level. Access to the filler and fueling control panel was through a forward swinging hinged access door in the lower surface of the wing's leading edge.

At 50 psi, the overall refueling rate was 375 gallons per minute. A fill control panel, with repeater fuel-quantity indicators, power control switch, and fill-valve control switches was located adjacent to the fill adapter. This control panel eliminated the need for personnel in the cockpit during fueling operations.

Overwing filling points were also provided for each main tank. Each tank was filled through a separate line regulated by a slow-closing (2 second) D-C electric shutoff valve. In the main tanks, automatic shut-off was provided by two float switches, wired in series, in each tank. The supplemental tank fill valve system was operated by a single float switch in each tank.

In addition to the automatic system, each fill valve can be operated by a switch on the fill panel or manually by an override lever on the valve. These alternates permitted manual filling to any level, even when the automatic system was inoperative.

Defueling was accomplished through the fueling panel by opening a manual defueling valve and operating a booster pump on the tank. A tank can also be defueled to the level of the fill line outlets by applying suction at the fill adapter. This system also expedited transfer of fuel from one tank to another while the aircraft was on the ground.

C-9 FUEL CAPACITY	
Left Wing	1,386 Gallons
Right Wing	1,386 Gallons
Center Wing	907 Gallons
Forward Fuselage	1,250 Gallons
Aft Fuselage	1,000 Gallons
Total Fuel	5,929 Gallons

Below, the C-9's single - point refueling receptacle and controls were located beneath the right wing about mis-span and just aft of the leading edge. (Harry Gann)

LANDING GEAR SYSTEM COMPONENTS

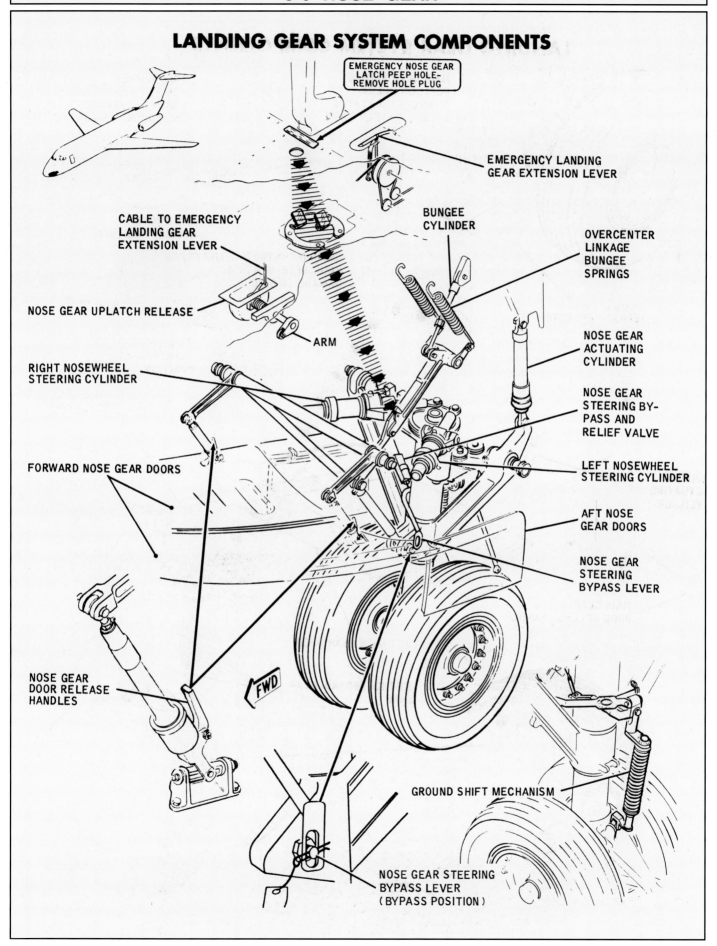

EMERGENCY NOSE GEAR LATCH PEEP HOLE-REMOVE HOLE PLUG

EMERGENCY LANDING GEAR EXTENSION LEVER

CABLE TO EMERGENCY LANDING GEAR EXTENSION LEVER

BUNGEE CYLINDER

OVERCENTER LINKAGE BUNGEE SPRINGS

NOSE GEAR UPLATCH RELEASE

ARM

NOSE GEAR ACTUATING CYLINDER

RIGHT NOSEWHEEL STEERING CYLINDER

NOSE GEAR STEERING BY-PASS AND RELIEF VALVE

FORWARD NOSE GEAR DOORS

LEFT NOSEWHEEL STEERING CYLINDER

AFT NOSE GEAR DOORS

NOSE GEAR STEERING BYPASS LEVER

NOSE GEAR DOOR RELEASE HANDLES

FWD

GROUND SHIFT MECHANISM

NOSE GEAR STEERING BYPASS LEVER (BYPASS POSITION)

The C-9 landing gear was a conventional tricycle arrangement with fully retractable components. Retraction and extension of all gear and doors was accomplished hydraulically by the right hydraulic system. The inboard main gear doors and forward nose gear doors close after gear extension to reduce cabin noise.

Each landing gear utilized an oleo-pneumatic shock strut with fixed axles and dual wheels. Each main landing gear wheel was equipped with thermal fuse plugs to prevent overheating.

Braking was accomplished by hydraulically operated multiple disc brakes for each main gear wheel. Each brake had two sets of pistons , independently operated by separate 3000 psi hydraulic systems. Separate hydraulic anti-skid valves were provided for each system so that each brake would provide redundancy in case of hydraulic system failure.

Nose wheel steering was accomplished hydraulically by two steering cylinders directly coupled to the nose gear shock strut. Each steering cylinder was powered by a separate hydraulic system and was controlled through separate, coordinated steering valves. Steering inputs were fed through the rudder-control system for turns up to 17° in each direction; for turns up to 82° in each direction, inputs are through the nose-wheel steering system. The 82° steering capability allows a full 180° turnaround on a taxiway of 78.8 feet.

LANDING GEAR SYSTEM COMPONENTS

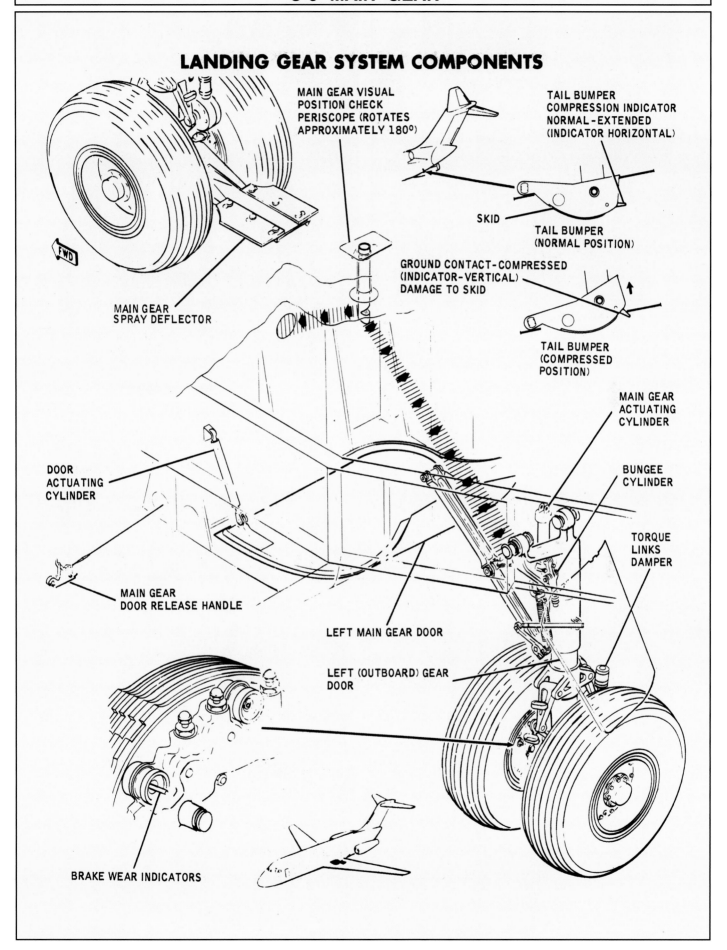

MAIN GEAR VISUAL POSITION CHECK PERISCOPE (ROTATES APPROXIMATELY 180°)

TAIL BUMPER COMPRESSION INDICATOR NORMAL-EXTENDED (INDICATOR HORIZONTAL)

SKID

TAIL BUMPER (NORMAL POSITION)

MAIN GEAR SPRAY DEFLECTOR

GROUND CONTACT-COMPRESSED (INDICATOR-VERTICAL) DAMAGE TO SKID

TAIL BUMPER (COMPRESSED POSITION)

MAIN GEAR ACTUATING CYLINDER

DOOR ACTUATING CYLINDER

BUNGEE CYLINDER

TORQUE LINKS DAMPER

MAIN GEAR DOOR RELEASE HANDLE

LEFT MAIN GEAR DOOR

LEFT (OUTBOARD) GEAR DOOR

BRAKE WEAR INDICATORS

C-9 MAIN GEAR

Above, main gear wheel well looking inboard. (Harry Gann) At right, right main gear looking forward. The blue item between the tires was the torque links damper. (Ginter) Bottom, right main gear looking aft. (Ginter)

C-9 AUXILLARY POWER UNIT (APU)

The APU was an onboard source of pneumatic and electric power. It freed the C-9B from any dependence on ground power equipment. The unit was a gas turbine engine (AiResearch Model GTCP8598D APU) that supplied pneumatic requirements for cabin air conditioning and engine starting as well as 40KVA of electric power for the operation of all normal aircraft systems. This unit was also operable in flight as an alternate source of electric power. It was self-starting and was controlled from the pilot's compartment.

The APU was located inside the airplane, aft of the pressure bulkhead. It was installed in a fixed, fireproof, sound-attenuated container mounted transversely on the lower centerline inlet; compartment cooling inlet and APU exhaust ducts were all sound treated to minimize noise. The exhaust was discharged overboard, above the right main engine pylon, to further reduce exhaust noise.

As with the main engine, installation design of the APU incorporated hoisting provisions for the entire demountable APU package or the electrical generator. Inspection and servicing were facilitated by two large doors on the bottom of the APU enclosure. These features made it unnecessary to remove the APU to change components or perform normal service operations.

At top right, APU location. At right, APU. Bottom right, left fuselage APU door open for inspection. (all Harry Gann) Below, closed left and right APU doors and tail skid. (Ginter)

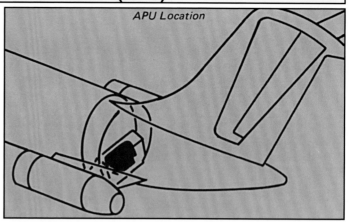

APU Location

JT8D-9A TURBOFAN ENGINE

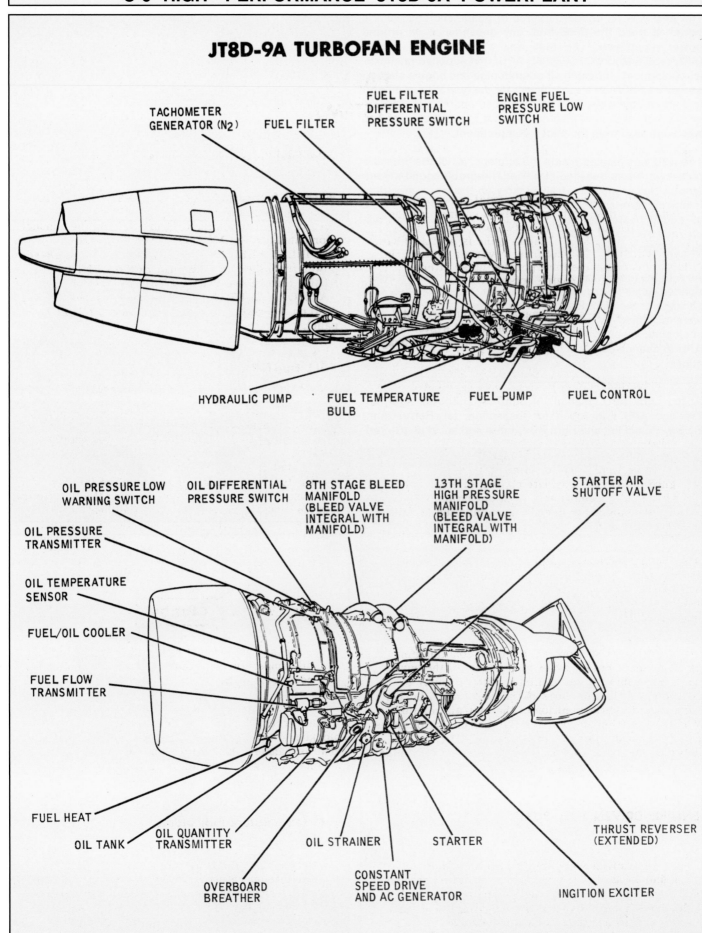

TACHOMETER GENERATOR (N_2)

FUEL FILTER

FUEL FILTER DIFFERENTIAL PRESSURE SWITCH

ENGINE FUEL PRESSURE LOW SWITCH

HYDRAULIC PUMP

FUEL TEMPERATURE BULB

FUEL PUMP

FUEL CONTROL

OIL PRESSURE LOW WARNING SWITCH

OIL DIFFERENTIAL PRESSURE SWITCH

8TH STAGE BLEED MANIFOLD (BLEED VALVE INTEGRAL WITH MANIFOLD)

13TH STAGE HIGH PRESSURE MANIFOLD (BLEED VALVE INTEGRAL WITH MANIFOLD)

STARTER AIR SHUTOFF VALVE

OIL PRESSURE TRANSMITTER

OIL TEMPERATURE SENSOR

FUEL/OIL COOLER

FUEL FLOW TRANSMITTER

FUEL HEAT

OIL TANK

OIL QUANTITY TRANSMITTER

OVERBOARD BREATHER

OIL STRAINER

CONSTANT SPEED DRIVE AND AC GENERATOR

STARTER

THRUST REVERSER (EXTENDED)

INGITION EXCITER

C-9 HIGH - PERFORMANCE JT8D-9A POWERPLANT

The C-9 aircraft was powered by two-axial-flow, bypass, turbfan, Pratt & Whitney JT8D-9A engines flat rated at 14,500 lbs static takeoff thrust at sea level up to 84° F. Each engine was equipped with a hydraulically actuated thrust reverser system. Static reverse thrust was approximately 30 to 35 percent of the forward thrust. In addition, each engine incorporated noise attenuation treatment to lesson engine noise levels.

The combustion section of the engine contained nine burner cans. Fuel nozzles at the front of the burner cans spray fuel for rapid mixing with air prior to combustion. Igniter plugs in the number 4 and number 7 burner cans provided initial ignition of the fuel-air mixture. When combustion occurs, the flame propagation tubes carry combustion to all burner cans.

The engine was started from a pneumatic ground cart, by its own self-contained APU, or by cross bleed.

Engine accessories include an air turbine starter, a hydraulic pump, a constant speed drive, and a 40 KVA generator. The accessories were grouped for maximum accessibility and were arranged so that individual components could be removed for maintenance without disturbing adjacent units.

The engine had a two-piece, quick-opening split cowl which gave easy access to all components. The right and left units were demountable and were designed for maximum commonality. The only major components which were not common were the nose cowls and the starter ducts.

The engine nacelles were supported from horizontal pylons by vibration-isolating side mount systems. The nose cowls were canted inboard to minimize drag. The nacelles were isolated from the fuselage by a firewall within the pylon and by a secondary fireseal at the pylon fuselage interface. To provide additional protection, the secondary fireseal extended above and below the pylon on the fuselage surface. To achieve necessary nacelle compartmentation, a fireseal was installed aft of the rear engine mount and provided separation of the accessory compartment from the reverser section. The nacelle ventilation system was designed to provide adequate cooling of the engine and accessories for ground and flight operation.

CHARACTERISTICS OF THE PRATT AND WHITNEY JT8D ENGINES		
Takeoff Thrust, Sea Level Static	lb	14,500
Maximum Ambient Temperature for Sea Level Static Takeoff Thrust	°F	84
Design Bypass Ratio		1.05
Takeoff Turbine Inlet Temperature	°F	1,931
Inlet Diameter	in.	42.5
Length	in.	120
Bare Weight		3,218
Design Compressor Pressure Ratio		16.5:1
Cruise Performance — Uninstalled at 30,000 ft at M = 0.80		
A. Max Cruise Thrust	lb	4,525
TSFC	lb/hr/lb	0.801
B. Min TSFC	lb/hr/lb	0.790
Thrust	lb	3,750

Above, empty C-9 engine bay looking up and forward. (Ginter) Below left, open engine nacelle on the right side of a C-9. Below right, C-9 engine with the thrust reverser deployed. (both photos Harry Gann)

C-9 WEATHER RADAR

The weather radar system provided visual indication of precipitation areas out to a 180-mile range so that turbulence associated with heavy rainfall areas can be avoided. The plan-position indicator (PPI) on the forward pedestal shows the range, azimuth, and magnitude of precipitaion areas. This allows the pilot to distinguish corridors of relatively calm air when flying through storm conditions. The system also provided for ground mapping and terrain avoidance by displays on the indicator. The system consisted of a radar antenna with drive and stabilization mechanisms mounted in the nose radome, a receiver-transmitter unit mounted in the forward accessory compartment, a control panel, and an indicator. A bright, visible display of weather and ground targets that were readable under all normal ambient lighting conditions without use of a viewing hood were shown on the indicator. The system contained self-test circuits that permitted on the ground or inflight system testing. (photo Harry Gann)

C-9 LEADING EDGE SLAT SYSTEM

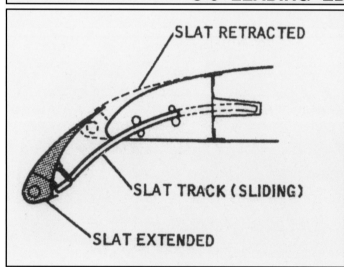

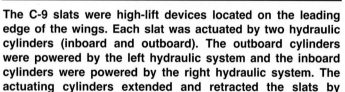

The C-9 slats were high-lift devices located on the leading edge of the wings. Each slat was actuated by two hydraulic cylinders (inboard and outboard). The outboard cylinders were powered by the left hydraulic system and the inboard cylinders were powered by the right hydraulic system. The actuating cylinders extended and retracted the slats by means of a closed cable and track system. Slat response should be fully extended or retracted. Normally, the slats operate by pressure from both hydraulic systems, but will continue to operate, at a reduced hinge moment adequate for normal extension, with pressure from a single hydraulic system. (both photos Ginter)

C-9 FLAP SYSTEM DOUBLE AND TRIPLE SLOTTED

For most of the flaps' length, the C-9 flaps were the double-slotted type that move aft and down. However, the last 3-or-4 feet before the fuselage were triple-slotted flaps. The double-slotted flaps were actuated by two hydraulic cylinders (inboard and outboard). The out-board cylinders received pressure from the left hydraulic system, and the inboard cylinders received pressure from the right hydraulic system. The flaps were normally operated by both hydraulic systems, but they continued to operate at a slower rate due to a reduced hinge moment which was sufficient to provide full flaps with a single hydraulic system. The flap control handle had detents at UP, 0, 5, 15, 25, 40, 50° positions.

Below, triple-slotted flaps fully deployed. (Harry Gann) At right, inboard double-slotted flap hinge. At right bottom, out-board double-slotted flap hinge. (both photos Ginter)

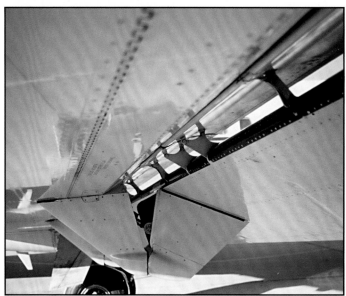

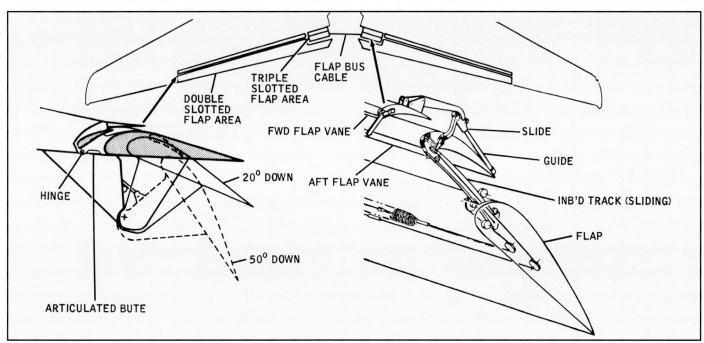

DOUBLE SLOTTED FLAP AREA

TRIPLE SLOTTED FLAP AREA

FLAP BUS CABLE

FWD FLAP VANE

AFT FLAP VANE

SLIDE

GUIDE

INB'D TRACK (SLIDING)

FLAP

HINGE

20° DOWN

50° DOWN

ARTICULATED BUTE

USAF VC-9C VIP TRANSPORT

The Air Force ordered three plush VIP transports based on the DC-9-32, designated VC-9C. These were S/Nos 73-1681, 73-1682, and 73-1683. All three entered service in 1975 and were assigned to the 89th MAW, at Andrews AFB, MD, until being re-assigned to the 932nd AW at Scott AFB, IL. In addition to the plush interior, the VC-9C had extended-range fuel tanks which provided for a 2,900 mile range. They also had a special communications suite installed when used by the vice president as "Air Force Two".

The three aircraft were frequently used as "Air Force Two" by vice presidents: Walter Mondale, George H.W. Bush, Dan Quayle, Al Gore, and Dick Cheney. They were also employed by America's First Ladies: Rosalynn Carter, Nancy Reagan, Barbara Bush, Hillary Clinton, Laura Bush, and Michelle Obama. Sometimes they even functioned as "Air Force One" when presidents needed access to smaller airports and were utilized by Ronald Reagan, George H.W. Bush, Bill Clinton, and George W. Bush.

The three aircraft were retired in 2011 and all three are now preserved in museums: 73-1681 is on display at the Castle Air Museum in Atwater, CA; 73-1682 is preserved at the Air Mobility Command Museum, Dover AFB, DE; 73-1683 is displayed at the Evergreen Aviation and Space Museum, McMinnville, OR.

Above, 89th MAW VC-9C, S/N 73-1681, early cutaway illustration. (Harry Gann) Bottom, 89th MAW VC-9C, S/N 73-1681, in flight near Andrews AFB. (Harry Gann)

Above, 89th MAW VC-9C, S/N 73-1681 and 73-1682, at Andrews AFB. (Phil Friddell collection) Below, two views of S/N 73-1682 in flight. (both Harry Gann)

Above, VC-9C radio room including SAT-COM controls. Above right, VC-9C lavatory. Below and bottom right, forward conference lounge. Bottom left, galley. (Air Mobility Command Museum/USAF)

Above, passenger cabin looking aft. Below, passenger cabin looking forward. Aircraft was set up for 42 seats. (USAF)

Above, VC-9C, S/N 73-1683, at MCAS El Toro, CA, in May 1977. (William Swisher) Below, VC-9C, S/N 73-1683 on display at the Evergreen Air and Space Museum, McMinnville, OR. (Paul Minert collection) Bottom, VC-9C, S/N 73-1683. (Ginter collection)

US Navy / US Marine C-9Bs / DC-9s

The Navy and Marines operated 17 contract built C-9Bs and 14 leased or purchased used DC-9 airliners (most modified for cargo) for a total of 31 aircraft.

These were: 159113, 159114, 159115, 159116, 159117, 159118, 159119, 159120, 160046, 160047, 160048, 160049, 160050, 160051, 161266, 161529, 161530, 162390, 162391, 162392, 162393, 162753, 162754, 163208, 163511, 163512, 163513, 164605, 164606, 164607, and 164608.

A 32nd aircraft, a DC-9-31, was assigned BuNo 168277, but was not directly utilized by the Navy Department. It was operated by the Federal Government out of China Lake as N932ML "Firebird II" from 2003-2006 and in October 2013-2021

At right and below, seen here is NC-9D, BuNo 168277, flown by Raytheon out of Mojave, CA, as N879AD on 23 October 2015. The aircraft is used in their missile systems development. (Craig Kaston)

by Raytheon as NC-9D with bogus civil registration of N879AD.

The first 8 C-9Bs built were intially assigned to VR-1 on the East Coast and VR-30 on the West Coast. In a 1976 reorganization of the reserves, it was decided to make the C-9B fleet a total reserve force with VR-1's "JK" and VR-30's "RW" aircraft equipping the first few squadrons. Eventually, a total of 11 reserve squadrons flew the C-9B. These were: VR-46 "JS", VR-51 "RV", VR-52 "JT", VR-55 "RU", VR-56 "JU", VR-57 "RX", VR-58 "JV", VR-59 "RY", VR-60 "RT", VR-61 "RS" and VR-62 "JW". A full complement of Skytrain IIs was four per squadron, a number

not always achieved.

VR-56, VR-58, and VR-59 all participated in the invasion of Grenada from 25 October to 2 November 1983. During the Gulf War, 10 C-9B squadrons were involved. These were: VR-51, VR-52, VR-55, VR-56, VR-57, VR-58, VR-59, VR-60, VR-61 and VR-62.

C-9B Testiamonial by LCDR Rick Morgan

"The Navy Reserve's C-9B fleet did tremendous work with little recognition over the years. The fleet used them to routinely move whole squadrons between places and they did so, both people and cargo, in a safe fashion. I shudder to think what the loss of one of these birds would've had on a unit's ability to operate. I had a lot of flights on C-9Bs on both coasts, frequently moving from a base to a carrier's location. VR-61 at Whidbey moved a lot of our EA-6B squadrons to places like North Island where we'd go aboard our carrier. At the end of deployments they brought our troops home to reunite them with their families. They did great work with little notice."

FLEET TACTICAL SUPPORT SQUADRON ONE, VR-1
FLEET LOGISTICS SUPPORT WING DETACHMENT WASHINTON DC
FLEET LOGISTIC SUPPORT SQUADRON ONE, VR-1 "STAR LIFTERS"

VR-1, the first of thirteen transport squadrons established under the Naval Air Transport Service (NATS) during WWII, was established at NAS Norfolk, VA, on 9 March 1942. The squadron operated R4Ds and R5Ds and was operating C-118s, C-130s, and TA-3Bs when the C-9Bs were acquired.

The initial eight C-9Bs were divided up equally between VR-1 (Atlantic) and VR-30 (Pacific). VR-1 received its first C-9B, BuNo 159117 ("City of Norfolk"), on 9 May 1973. BuNos

159118 ("City of Jacksonville"), 159119, and 159120 ("City of Virginia Beach"), were received on 4 July 1973, 18 August 1973 and 31 October 1973 respectively. Two more C-9Bs were acquired in 1975-1976. BuNo 160048 ("City of New Orleans") was received on 19 August 1975 and 160049 on 27 February 1976.

When the Navy established the reserve Logistic Squadrons in July 1976, the squadron's C-9Bs were transferred out to these squadrons. The first to go were: BuNos 159117

and 160048 on 1 July 1976; 159119 on 2 July 1976; 160049 on 1 April 1978; and 159118 and 159119 on 1 September 1978. The squadron was disestablished and re-organized as Fleet Logistics Support Wing Detachment, Washington DC, on 1 October 1978.

Below, VR-1 C-9Bs, BuNo 159118 JK/118 "City of Charleston" and 159119 JK/119, in flight. (Mark Aldrich collection)

64

On 1 May 1997, Fleet Logistics Support Wing Detachment, Washington, DC, was redesignated Fleet Logistic Support Squadron One (VR-1) "Star Lifters" under the Commander, Naval Air Reserve Force. The new VR-1's first CO was CDR Wayne Chechila. Its mission was to provide Executive Air Transportation for Navy Department Executives both military and civilian in the Washington, DC, area. It operated out of NAF Washington (Andrews AFB) and primarily used C-1As and C-20Ds.

Two C-9Bs were added in May 2016, these were BuNos 161529 and 161530. Both aircraft were retired in April 2018.

Above, VR-1 C-9B, BuNo 159117 JK/117 "City of Norfolk", at Naples, Italy. (Carlo Tripodi via Angelo Romano) Below, VR-1 C-9B, BuNo 159118 JK/118 "City of Jacksonville", at Naples, Italy, in January 1978. (Giorgio Salerno via Angelo Romano) Bottom, VR-1 C-9B, BuNo 160048 JK/121 "City of New Orleans", in April 1976 at NAS Alameda, CA. (Angelo Romano collection)

FLEET LOGISTICS SQUADRON THIRTY, VR-30 / VRC-30 "PROVIDERS"

VR-30 was established at NAS Alameda, CA, from elements of VRC-50 in 1960. It was initially equipped with C-131 Samaritans and C-1A Trader COD aircraft. The unit was awarded the Meritorious Unit Commendation in 1967 and was utilized during the Apollo X, XI, XII, and XVI recovery operations. VR-30's C-1As supported CTF-77 operations in Vietnam out of Danang in 1969-1970.

In 1971, the squadron received two North American CT-39 Sabreliners for high-speed executive airlift before receiving the first of four C-9B Skytrain IIs on 9 May 1973 while under the command of CDR T.G. Campbell.

VR-30 received the first four C-9Bs delivered: BuNo 159113, 9 May; 159114, 14 June; 159116, 28 July; and 159116, 15 September. In 1975/1976, two more Skytrain IIs were acquired. These were BuNos 160050 and 160051. BuNos 159113, 159115 and 160050 were transferred out in April 1976.

Beginning on 25 July 1976, squadron C-9Bs were tasked as "Pathfinder" aircraft for Marine A-4 Skyhawk squadrons that were TransPacing to and from Japan. The first TransPac was "Operation Keyjoint". Two of VR-30's Skytrain IIs, utilizing 8 pilots and 12 enlisted air-

men, led VMA-223 Skyhawks from MCAS El Toro, CA, to MCAS Kaneohe Bay, HI, to Wake Island and finally to MCAS Iwakuni. The A-4s had to aerial refuel at least once every leg to be able to fly nonstop. On the return trip, the C-9Bs flew as Pathfinders for VMA-211, leading the squadron of A-4s back to MCAS El Toro. Once back in CONUS, VR-30 was congratulated for its work by the Commandant of the Marine Corps GEN Louis H. Wilson.

As a result of the success of TransPac Keyjoint, VR-30 Skytrain IIs were tasked with other Pathfinder missions to WESTPAC. These have

---

Below, VR-30 C-9B, BuNo 159113 RW/113, on 19 January 1975. (Fred Roos) Bottom, VR-30 C-9B, BuNo 159114 RW/114, at NAS Fallon, NV, on 19 January 1975. (William Swisher)

included squadrons from the A-4, A-6, A-7, F-4, and AV8 communities. The long range C-9B had proved itself to be extremely reliable and was equipped with Inertial Navigation Omega which made it the perfect choice to lead Navy and Marine squadrons across thousands of miles of water where there was no navigational aids.

On 1 October 1978, VR-30 was redesignated VRC-30, prior to which the C-9Bs were transferred out. BuNo 160051 departed in March and BuNos 159114 and 159116 left in September.

In February 1980, the squadron became the C-12 Fleet Replacement Squadron and in late 1985 the C-2A Greyhound replaced the squadron's

Above, VR-30 C-9B, BuNo 159115 RW/115, at NAS Alameda, CA, on 11 October 1975. (Tom Chee) Bottom, VR-30 C-9B, BuNo 159116 RW/116, in 1973. (Harry Gann)

six C-1As. In 1994, VRC-50's assets and C-2s were absorbed into VRC-30.

Above, VR-30 C-9B, BuNo 160050 RW/050. Note crossed flags on fusalage side. (Paul Minert collection) Below, VR-30 C-9B, BuNo 160051 RW/051, in February 1978. (Paul Minert collection)

FLEET LOGISTICS SQUADRON FORTY - SIX, VR-46 "EAGLES"

With the re-organization of the reserves in 1970, Fleet Logistics Squadron Forty-Six (VR-46) was established at NAS Atlanta, GA, with Douglas C-118 transport aircraft.

The C-118's were slowly replaced with C-9Bs starting with BuNo 163208 the "City of Marietta" on 14 June 1984. Two more were received in 1986: BuNo 163512 "City of Atlanta", on 15 May; and BuNo 163513, on 16 June. In 1994 four more C-9Bs were acquired. These were: BuNo 159113; 159114, "City of Atlanta"; 161529, "City of Acworth"; and 163511. All of the unit's C-9Bs were transferred out by 1996. However, one last Skytrain II was assigned to VR-46 in 1996. It was BuNo 161266 "City of Woodstock'" which was operated until 2009.

Below, VR-46 C-9B, BuNo 159114 JS/114 "City of Atlanta", at Naples, Italy, on 7 January 1999. (Giorgio Salerno via Angelo Romano)

On 5 October 2007, LCDR Edmonds and crew flew 161266 from NAS Atlanta, GA, to NAS Key West, FL. During this flight the aircraft and crew logged VA-46's 100,000th mishap-free C-9B flight hour.

Above, VR-46 C-9B, BuNo 161266 JS/266 "City of Woodstock", landing at Naples, Italy, on 8 January 1996. (Giorgio Salerno via Angelo Romano) Below, VR-46 C-9B, BuNo 161529 JS/529 "City of Acworth", at Naples, Italy, on 2 January 2001. (Chris Doherty) Below middle, VR-46 C-9B, BuNo 163208 JS/208 "City of Marietta", at Naples, Italy, on 4 January 1995. (Giorgio Salerno via Angelo Romano) Bottom, VR-46 C-9B, BuNo 163511 JS/511, in company with VR-52 C-9B, BuNo 163036 JT/036, in October 1997. (David Brown via Paul Minert)

Above, VR-46 C-9B, BuNo 163512 JS/512 "City of Atlanta", in September 1986. (David Brown via Paul Minert)

FLEET LOGISTICS SQUADRON FIFTY - ONE, VR-51 "FLAMIN HOOKERS"

"Village of Glenview", was accepted on 6 January 1984 and 162754 RV/754 "The Windy City", was acquired on 1 February 1984. 162753 left the squadron in 1995 and 162754 was withdrawn in 1993. The squadron operated a third C-9B from its home base at Glenview. It was BuNo 163208 RV/208, from 1996 through 9 December 2001.

Below, VR-51 C-9B, BuNo 162753 RV/753 "Village of Glenville", at McDonnell. (Paul Minert collection) Bottom, VR-51 C-9B, BuNo 162754 RV/754 "The Windy City", at NAS Oceana, VA, on 10 October 1987. (Jim Sullivan)

With the re-organization of the reserves in 1970, VR-51 was established at NAS Alameda, CA, with C-118Bs. It maintained detachments at NAS Whidbey Island, WA, and NAS Glenview, IL. In 1984, two C-9Bs replaced the C-118Bs based at Glenview. BuNo 162753 RV/753

FLEET LOGISTICS SQUADRON FIFTY - TWO VR-52 "TASKMASTERS"

Fleet Logistics Squadron Fifty-Two (VR-52) was established on 1 June 1972 at NAS Willow Grove, PA, and was equipped with C-118Bs. The squadron also maintained detachments at NAF Detroit, MI, and NAF Washington, DC. In December 1978, the C-118Bs at Washington, DC, were replaced with C-131H turbo-props and the detachment was re-designated VR-48 in 1980.

In September 1982, four leased civilian DC-9s were delivered to VR-52's Detachment Detroit and given BuNos 162390, 162391, 162392 and 162393. However, one day later, two each were re-assigned to VR-60 and VR-61.

On 13 September 1984, VR-52 was assigned C-9B, BuNo 163036 "City of Philadelphia", a civilian DC-9-32CF purchased by the Navy. After conversion, it was operated by the squadron until May 1998. A second civilian DC-9-32F was accepted on 27 August 1984 as BuNo 163037 "City of Willow Grove". The C-9Bs were operated until 2000 and 2003 respectively. 163036 had previously been operated by Overseas National Airways, Air Canada, Southern Airways and Republic Airways. 163037 was operated by Alitalia, Overseas National Airways, and Evergreen International Airways.

The squadron received the 1991 CNO Safety Award and the 1992 and 1998 Congressman Bill Chappell Award for Operational Excellence in Fleet Logistics Operations over a 20 year period. Also in 1992, VR-52 was awarded the Noel Davis Award (Battle E). In 1993, the squadron was awarded the 1993 James M. Holcombe Award for the best maintenance department in the Wing. A Navy Unit Commendation for support of the Sixth Fleet during Operations Desert Shield/Storm and Operation Provide Comfort and in 1997 the COMPFLELOGSUPPWING Training Excellence Award.

The eighth C-9B built, BuNo 159120, was acquired and operated by VR-52 from 1993 through 1995.

In June 1983, two civilian DC-9-33s were purchased. They received BuNos 162753 "Spirit of Somerset County" and 162754. They were re-assigned to VR-52 from 1994 to 2003.

In July 2002, C-9B, BuNo 160048 "City of Philadelphia", was received as was Its sistership, BuNo 160049. In December 2002-2005, both aircraft took part in the squadron's Fantasy Flight to the North Pole on December 4th. This was in combination with the Make-A-Wish Foundation for about 75 disabled and health challenged children living with life-threatening medical conditions. The aircraft were stocked with elevs and Santa for the

---

Below, VR-52 C-9B, BuNo 162753 JT/753, "The Spirit of Valley Forge" (later named "Sumerset County"). (Paul Minert collection) Bottom, VR-52 C-9B, BuNo 162754 JT/754. (Norris Graser via Paul Minert)

30-to-45 minute flight to the North Pole. During the flight the following activities were available: buffet lunch, petting zoo, movie lounge, face painting, animal ballon making, fun house and pitch booth.

In June and November 2004, BuNo 160049 was tasked to assist the Patuxent River Test Center develop the PMA-207 infrared imaging (IR) device. The June 2004 utilization was a set-up verification procedure for an IR signature of a C-9B with the installation of an Advanced Range Data System (ARDS) followed by several ground tests of the GPS and TACAN antennas. In November 2004 flight testing commenced. The purpose for the flights was to amass flight information to be utilized in designs of

future defense against MANPAD (Manual Portable Air Defense) systems. The purpose of the tests was to determine if it was possible and cost effective to equip the C-9B with shoulder launched missile protection. BuNo 160048 was retired on 5 June 2012 and 160049 on 16 November 2011.

At top, VR-52 C-9B, BuNo 163036 JT/036, landing in October 1985. (Ron Picciani) Above, VR-52 C-9B, BuNo 163037 JT/037, landing in October 1985. (Ron Picciani) Below, VR-52 C-9B, BuNo 160048 JT/0048 "City of Willow Grove". (Paul Minert collection) Bottom, VR-52 C-9B, BuNo 160049 JT/049, at Malta. (Mark Aldrich collection)

FLEET LOGISTICS SQUADRON FIFTY-FIVE, VR-55 "BICENTENNIAL MINUTEMEN"

On 1 September 1974, Reserve Squadron VR-1020 was established at NAS Alameda, CA. It utilized the assets including the C-9Bs assigned to VR-30. On 1 April 1976, VR-1020 at NAS Alameda, CA, was redesignated VR-55 and was assigned three of VR-30's C-9Bs. These were BuNos 159113, 159115 and 160050. 159115 was operated until 8 April 1978 while 159113 stayed in service with VR-55 until 1993 and 160050 left for VR-58 on 29 August 1979. It was replaced by 159120 on 1 September 1978 which transferred out in 1993. 160051 was acquired on 22 March 1978 and was retired in 1993.

The squadron won the Noel Davis Award for 1991 and in 1993 the Minutemen transitioned to the C-130T Hercules and transferred to NAS Point Mugu, CA.

Below, VR-55 C-9B, BUNO 159113 RU/113 "City of Alameda", at NAS Alameda on 8 November 1979. (Tom Chee)

Below, VR-55 C-9B, BUNO 159113 RU/113 "City of Alameda", at NAS Alameda on 21 March 1981. (Tom Chee) Bottom, VR-55 C-9B, BuNo 159115 RU/115, at NAS Alameda, CA, on 2 November 1977. (William Swisher)

At top, VR-55 C-9B, BUNO 159120 RU/120 "City of Oakland", at NAS Alameda on 4 April 1981. (Tom Chee) Above, VR-55 C-9B, BUNO 159120 RU/120 "City of Oakland", landing. (Carl Porter via Paul Minert) Below, VR-55 C-9B, BUNO 160050 RU/050 "Alameda", at NAS Miramar, CA, on 12 February 1977. (Roy Lock via Tom Chee) Bottom, VR-55 C-9B, BUNO 160051 RU/051, on 15 May 1981. (Tom Chee)

FLEET LOGISTIC SQUADRON FIFTY - SIX, VR-56 "GLOBEMASTERS"

VR-56 was established on 1 July 1976 at NAS Norfolk, VA. It was allocated three C-9Bs: BuNos 159117 "City of Norfolk" ("City of Pensacola" after August 2006) and 160048 "City of New Orleans" were acquired on 1 July 1976, 159119 "City of Charleston" was received on 2 July 1976. 160048 was transferred to VR-58 on 29 August 1978 and replaced by 159118 "City of Chesapeake" on 1 September 1978. A forth C-9B, BuNo 159120 "City of Virginia Beach", was added in 1995.

The squadron received the 1979 CNO Safety Award and was transfered to NAS Oceana, VA, in August 2006.

In early 2010, VR-56 was notified it would receive C-40As 10, 11, and 12 to replace its C-9Bs. Following this, 159119 was retired on 22 May 2010, 159120 on 6 July 2010 and 159117 in October 2010. BuNo 159118 was retained until November 2011 before being retired. By 2012, BuNo 159120 had been put on display at the Pima Air and Space Museum.

Below, VR-56 C-9B, BuNo 159117 JU/117 "City of Norfolk", in 1994. (Mike Wilson collection) Bottom, VR-56 C-9B, BuNo 159118 JU/118 "City of Chesapeake", at Naples, Italy, in July 2005. (Giorgio Salerno)

Above, VR-56 C-9B, BuNo 159119 JU/119 "City of Charleston", at NAF Andrews in 1989. (B. Tourville via Mike Wilson collection) Below, VR-56 C-9B, BuNo 159119 JU/119 "City of Charleston", landing at Naples, Italy. (Giorgio Salerno) Bottom, VR-56 C-9B, BuNo 159120 JU/120 "City of Virgina Beach", at Andrews AFB, on 26 February 2005. (Mark Aldrich collection)

Above, VR-56 C-9B, BuNo 160048 JU/048 "City of New Orleans", in flight in late 1976. Note upper wing codes. (Harry Gann) Below, BuNo 159117 after being preped for its retirement flight in November 2011. (Ginter collection) Bottom, BuNo 159120 at the Pima Air and Space Museum in November 2012. (Ginter)

Fleet Logistics Squadron Fifty-Seven (VR-57) was formally established at NAS North Island, CA, on 16 April 1978 with one C-9B, BuNo 159115 "City of San Diego" assigned while under the command of CDR W.J. Moyer. This aircraft flew three missions that day. The first was a flight to Oak Harbor, WA, two hours before the christening. The second was a local flight in California and the third repatriated 90 Naval Air Reservists to Arizona after their monthly drill weekend.

Two more C-9Bs were acquired on 1 September 1978. These were BuNos 159114 "City of Coronado" and 159116 "City of Long Beach" ("City of Temecula" in 1990 and "City of Sembach" 1991-1996).

In 1987 and 1990 the squadron was awarded the Noel Davis Trophy for the Reserve Force Squadron achieving the highest level of mobi-

Above, VR-57 C-9B, BuNo 159113 RX/113 "City of San Diego", lifting off. (Mark Aldrich collection) Below, VR-57 plaque. Bottom, VR-57 C-9B, BuNo 159114 RX/114 "City of Coronado", at NAS Alameda, CA, on 8 November 1979. (Tom Chee)

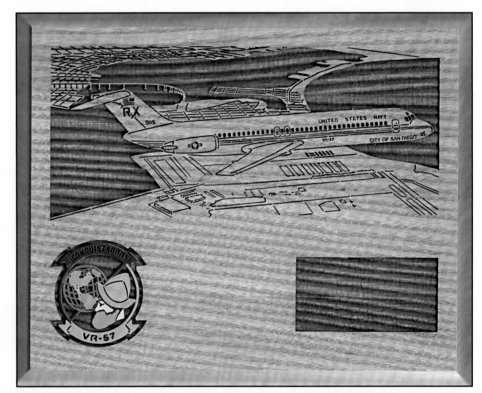

lization readiness. In 1983, 1988 and 1992, VR-57 received the CNO Safety Award and in 1988 the Commander, Fleet Logistics Support Wing's Retention Excellence Award. In December 1990, the squadron operated from Sembach AB, Germany, for four months during Operation Desert Shield. This result-ed in a Navy Unit Commendation and an Air Force Unit Commendation. During 1994, VR-57 flew 5,449 hours, transported 24,500 passengers, and carried 950,000 pounds of cargo.

In 2003, after 25-years of flying C-9Bs, the squadron had flown over 125,000 Class A mishap-free flight

Above, VR-57 C-9B, BuNo 159115 RX/115, over the Coronado Bay Bridge. (USN) Below, VR-57 C-9B, BuNo 159116 RX/116 "City of Long Beach", over the USS Ranger (CVA-61) in October 1981. (NMNA via J. Waarde)

hours. During 2003 alone, VR-57 had flown over 25,000 passengers and

carried 1.5 million pounds of cargo to worldwide destinations, including support of Operation Iraqi Freedom. VR-57 flew 425 flight hours, carried 953 passengers and delivered 300,500 pounds of cargo in March 2003 alone.

In the last half of the 1990s, BuNos 159114 and 159116 were transferred out and replaced with three others: BuNos 159113, 163512 "City of Coronado", and 164607 "City of Dublin". These three and BuNo 159115 were operated until replaced with C-40 aircraft.

At top, VR-57 C-9B, BuNo 159114 RX/114 "City of Coronado", at NAS Miramar on 26 July 1986 (Mark Morgan) Above, VR-57 C-9B, BuNo 159115 RX/115 "City of San Diego", at NAS Whidbey Island, WA, on 24 August 1985. (Mark Morgan) Below, VR-57 C-9B, BuNo 163512 RX/512 "City of Coronado". (Jerrod Wilkening via Paul Minert) Bottom, VR-57 C-9B, BuNo 164607, at Pima in November 2012. (Ginter)

Fleet Logistics Support Squadron Fifty-Eight (VR-58) was established at NAS Jacksonville, FL, on 1 November 1977. Formal ceremonies were held on 1 April 1978 when the first C-9B, BuNo 160049 "City of Jacksonville", was delivered. On 29 August 1979, an additional two aircraft, BuNos 160048 "City of New Orleans" ("City of Catania" 1991, "City of St. Augustine" 1993-1996), and 160050 "Spirit of America" ("Spirit of Orange Park" 1981-1988), were acquired.

VR-58 (VR-56 and VR-59) pro-

vided logistical support during Operation Urgent Fury, the invasion of Grenada, from 25 October through 2 November 1983. The purpose of the mission was to protect American citizens, including the rescuing of trapped medical students and to provide stability to the area at the invitation of the Organization of Eastern Caribbean States.

VR-58 was awarded the Noel Davis Trophy in August 1983 and August 1985. It also received the CNO Safety Award in August 1984.

In response to the Gulf War, VR-58 was mobilized and operated two C-9Bs from 27 December 1990 to 21 May 1991. The squadron operated from NAF Capodichino, Naples, and NAS Sigonella, Sicily. During this

Above, VR-58 C-9B, BuNo 160048 JV/048, landing in the early 1980s. (Mike Wilson collection) Below, VR-58 C-9B, BuNo 160049 JV/049 "City of Jacksonville", on 8 December 1979. (Tom Chee) Bottom, the first C-9B, BuNo 160049 JV/049, received by VR-58 over Jacksonville in April 1978. (Harry Gann)

period, the squadron flew 380 missions (2,700 flight hours), moving 2.5 million pounds of cargo and 11,000 passengers during the five-month deployment.

A fourth C-9B, BuNo 160051 "City of Orlando", was received on 11 October 1994. All four aircraft were replaced by C-40As.

Above, VR-58 C-9B, BuNo 160050 JV/050 "City of Orange Park", at NS Roosevelt Roads in 8 April 1982. (Tom Chee)

Below, VR-58 C-9B, BuNo 160048 JV/048 "City of Orange Park", at Naples, Italy. (Angelo Romano collection)

Bottom, VR-58 C-9B, BuNo 160050 JV/050 "City of Orange Park", at Naples, Italy. (Angelo Romano collection)

FLEET LOGISTIC SQUADRON FIFTY - NINE, VR-59 "LONE STAR EXPRESS"

Fleet Logistics Squadron Fifty-Nine (VR-59) was formally established at JRB Fort Worth, TX, on 1 October 1982 after obtaining its first C-9B, BuNo 161266 "City of Dallas", on 30 September. Two more C-9Bs, BuNos 161529 "City of Fort Worth" and 161530 "City of Grand Prairie", were acquired on 1 December 1982.

VR-59 (VR-56 and VR-58) provided logistical support during Operation Urgent Fury, the invasion of Grenada, from 25 October through 2 November 1983. The purpose of the mission was to protect American citizens, including the rescueing of trapped medical students and to provide stability to the area at the invitation of the Organization of Eastern Caribbean States.

VR-59 was awarded the 1986 Noel Davis Trophy for mobilization readiness and from 27 December 1990 to 21 May 1991, VR-59, along with nine other C-9B reserve squadrons, operated in the support of the Gulf War.

A fourth C-9B, BuNo 163208, was acquired in 1996. The squadron ceased operating C-9Bs on 1 October 2000 and became the first unit to operate the new Boeing C-40A replacement aircraft on 21 April 2001.

Below, VR-59 C-9B, BuNo 161266 RY/266 "City of Dallas", on 10 November 1984. (McGarry via Mike Wilson) Middle, VR-59 C-9B, BuNo 161529 RY/529 "City of Fort Worth", on 24 February 1983 at NAF Washington. (Don Linn) Bottom, VR-59 C-9B, BuNo 161530 RY/530 "City of Grand Prairie". (Jerrod Wilkening via Paul Minert)

Above, VR-59 C-9B, BuNo 163208 RY/208 "City of Arlington", in September 2000. (Bob Patterson, Jr, via Paul Minert)

FLEET LOGISTICS SQUADRON SIXTY, VR-60 "VOLUNTEER EXPRESS"

C-118-equipped VR-53 Detacthment NAS Dallas, TX, formed the nucleus for Fleet Logistic Squadron Sixty (VR-60). VR-60 was established at NAS Memphis, TN, on

3 October 1982 with two leased DC-9-31 airliners. BuNo 162390, "City of Memphis", was acquired on 29 September 1982 and was not equipped for cargo but was operated as an airliner without the cargo door conversion. It was originally flown by Ansett begining in 1967, then purchased by Marfreless on 27 September 1982 before being leased to the Navy on 29 September 1982. BuNo 162391, "City of Millington", was also owned by Ansett and purchased by Marfreless on 20 September 1982 before being leased by the Navy. Unlike 162390, 162391 was modified to C-9B standards and equipped with a cargo door. Both aircraft were returned to Marfreless in 1990, 162390 on 20 July and 162391

in November. The two aircraft were replaced by two used (ex Iberia) DC-9-33 airliners purchased from McDonnell Douglas. 164605, "City of Memphis", was acquired on 12 July 1990 and 164606, "City of Millington", was received on 23 August 1990. Both aircraft were transferred to VR-61 in 1994 when VR-60 was disestablished.

Below, VR-60 C-9B, BuNo 162390 RT/390, "City of Memphis" at NAF Andrews in October 1986. (Paul Minert collection) Bottom, VR-60 C-9B, BuNo 162391 RT/391, "City of Millington", at NAF Andrews on 5 September 1987. (A. Mongeon via Mike Wilson collection)

FLEET LOGISTICS SQUADRON SIXTY - ONE, VR-61. "ISLANDERS"

Fleet Logistic Squadron Sixty-One (VR-61) was established on 1 October 1982 at NAS Whidbey Island, WA, with two DC-9-31 leased aircraft acquired on 18 September 1982. These were BuNos 162392 "City of Seattle" and 162393 "City of Oak Harbor", originally owned by Ansett then purchased by Marfreless and leased to the Navy without the C-9B cargo modifications. They were

replaced with two DC-9-33 aircraft with C-9B cargo modifications that were purchased from McDonnell Douglas by the Navy on 1 August 1990. These two were previously owned by Iberia Airlines. They were BuNos 164607 "City of Seattle" and 164608 "City of Oak Harbor". In the fall of 1994, two more cargo modified DC-9-33 were acquired. These were BuNos 164605 "City of Everett" and 164606 "City of Bremerton", both received from VR-60.

In 1998, the four DC-9-33 aircraft were replaced with the first four C-9Bs built, BuNos 159113, 159114 "Spirit of Meg Ryan", 159115 and 159116 "City of Seattle". 160050 was also acquired about this same time.

Another ex-KLM DC-9 airliner was purchased by the Navy and utilized by VR-61 in 2002 through 2003. It was BuNo 162754 which was bailed to NASA on 9 August 2003 and registered N933NA.

In 2005, VR-61 carried 20,415 passengers and over 764,000 pounds of cargo, of which 4,688 flight hours were in direct support of Operations Noble Eagle, Iraqi Freedom and Enduring Freedom. In 2006, the squadron was maintaining a detachment of one aircraft at Atsugi, Japan, NAF Sigonella, Sicily, and NSA Bahrain, Oman. During the year they flew 14,730 passengers and transported 724,781 pounds of

Below, VR-61 C-9B, BuNo 162392 RS/392 "City of Seattle", at Nellis AFB in September 1985. (Paul Minert collection) Bottom, VR-61 C-9B, BuNo 162393 RS/393 "City of Oak Harbor", at NAS Whidbey Island in October 1985, one of four DC-9s leased by the Navy from the airlines. The other three were BuNos 162390, 162391 and 162392. Note that these were not fitted with a cargo door. (Rick Morgan)

cargo. They flew 4,599 hours of which 1,803 were in direct support of operations Noble Eagle, Enduring Freedom and Iraqi Freedom. During the 2007 winter holidays, VR-61 flew over 200 hours in direct support of Operations Enduring Freedom and Iraqi Freedom which included the transportation of over 600 passengers and 375,000 pounds of cargo.

In fiscal year 2013, VR-61 flew 3,742 hours carrying 11,498 passengers and over one million pounds of cargo. By 2013, the squadron had accumulated over 127,000 mishap-free flight hours and had received eight safety awards. In addition, during the Gulf War, the unit received a Meritorious Unit Commendation and

At top, VR-61 C-9B, BuNo 162754 RS/754 "City of Anacortes", in October 2002. (Paul Minert collection) Above, VR-61 C-9B, BuNo 164606 RS/606 "City of Bremerton", lifting off. (McCurdy via Paul Minert) Below, VR-61 C-9B, BuNo 164605 RS/605, taking-off in February 1998. (Paul Minert collection) Bottom, VR-61 C-9B, BuNo 164607 RS/607 "City of Seattle", landing on 24 July 2002. (Rich Rentrop)

At top, VR-61 C-9B, BuNo 164608 RS/608 "City of Oak Harbor", landing in October 2002. (Paul Minert collection) Above, VR-61 C-9B, BuNo 159113, on 12 May 2008. (Mark Aldrich collection) Below, VR-61 C-9B, BuNo 159114, in June 2007. (Paul Minert collection) Bottom, VR-61 C-9B, BuNo 159116 RS/116 "City of Seattle", landing in November 2003. (Paul Minert collection)

a Navy Unit Commendation. Also while flying the C-9B, two Congressman Bill Chappell awards, four Noel Davis Battle "E" awards, four retention awards and the James M. Holcombe Maintenance Award were garnished.

VR-61 was the last Navy squadron to fly the C-9B, with the last aircraft, BuNo 160050, departing the unit on 28 June 2014.

At left, the last Navy C-9B, BuNo 160050 RS/050 "Caboose", being retired at NAS Whidbey Island, WA, on 28 June 2014. (USN)

KUWAIT. AIR FORCE C-9Ks

The Kuwait Air Force ordered two DC-9-32CF aircraft designated C-9K in 1977. The two aircraft were assigned BuNos 160749 and 160750 and Kuwait Air Force KAF320 and KAF321 respectively. KAF320 was destroyed on the ground at Kuwait City on 2 October 1990 when Iraq invaded Kuwait.

In May 1998, KAF321 was sold to Comtran International and registered N724HB. Two years later it was sold to USA Jet Airlines where it was registered N205US.

After the Gulf War, the Kuwait Air Force ordered a DC-9-83 (MD-83) coded KAF26 to replace KAF320.

Below, Kuwait Air Force DC-9-83 (MD-83) KAF26. (Paul Minert collection)

FLEET LOGISTICS SQUADRON SIXTY - TWO, VR-62 "MOTOWNERS"

Fleet Logistics Support Squadron Sixty-Two (VR-62) was established on 1 July 1985 at NAF Detroit, MI. The squadron received two DC-9-32 aircraft that were being operated by Aero Transport Italian. The Navy took delivery of BuNo 163511 "City of Mount Clemens" on 23 September 1985 and 163513 "City of Detroit" on 21 January 1986. The two aircraft were operated until late 1994 when they were transferred to VR-46.

On 1 April 1994, the squadron transferred to NAS South Weymouth, MA, and transitioned to the C-130T Hercules. The first C-130T was received in January 1995.

Below, VR-62 C-9B, BuNo 163511 JW/511 "City of Mount Clemens", in August 1986. (Paul Minert collection) Middle, VR-62 C-9B, BuNo 163513 JW/513 "City of Detroit", at McChord AFB in June 1989. (E.F Jones via Paul Minert collection) Bottom, VR-62 C-9B, BuNo 163513 JW/513 "City of Detroit", in June 1989. (Paul Minert collection)

SOES / MARINE TRANSPORT SQUADRON ONE, VMR-1 "ROADRUNNERS"

The Marines' two C-9Bs, BuNos 160046 and 160047, were received in 1975 and stationed at MCAS Cherry Point, NC, and assigned to the Station Operations and Engineering Squadron (SOES). In 1997 SOES was redesignated Marine Transport Squadron One (VMR-1).

The squadron operated two C-9B Skytrain IIs, two UC-35D Cessna Encores, and three HH-46D Sea Knight helicopters. The squadron operated its C-9B and UC-35 aircraft as cargo and troop transports and as VIP transports. This included in-theatre suport during Operations Desert Shield and Desert Storm.

In 2014, the two C-9Bs were

replaced with BuNos 161529 and 161530 which were operated until 2017. In 2020 the U.S. Air Force acquired 161529 and is currently using it as a sensor test ship out of

Colorado Springs.

The squadron transferred to Joint

Above, Marine SOES C-9B, BuNo 160046, at MCAS Cherry Point, NC, on 2 January 1976. (Jim Sullivan) Below, SOES C-9B, BuNo 160046. (SDASM via Mark Aldrich)

Reserve Base Fort Worth, TX, in December 2017 and converted from the C-9B to the Boeing C-40A.

Above, subdued VMR-1 C-9B, BuNo 160046, at Andrews AFB, on 21 February 2004. (Stephen Miller) Above, SOES C-9B, BuNo 160047, at MCAS Cherry Point, NC, on 29 April 1975. (Jim Sullivan) Below, VMR-1 C-9B, BuNo 160047, at MCAS Cherry Point, NC, in 2002. (Mike Wilson) Bottom, VMR-1 C-9B, BuNo 160047 in subdued grey paint scheme upon retirement at AMARG in 2014. (Mark Aldrich collection)

NASA REDUCED GRAVITY C-9B, N932NA "VOMIT COMET"

The NASA C-9B, BuNo 162754 / N932NA (NASA 932), is the 9th in a series of planes used in the Reduced Gravity Program which started in 1957. The first three aircraft were C-131 / Convair 240-400s replaced by five Boeing KC-135s beginning in 1967. The last KC-135, NASA 931, flew its last flight on 29 October 2004 after being acquired in 1994. During its career it flew over 37,000 parabolas.

The C-9B was transferred from VR-61 at NAS Whidbey Island, WA,

Below, NASA N932NA "Vomit Comet" starts a parabolic flight. (NASA)

to NASA on 9 August 2003. Its mission is to provide NASA, government, and civil researchers a vehicle in which to perform their research in a reduced gravity environment. It also provides Heavy Aircraft Training (HAT) for astronaut pilots and use as a transport aircraft for other NASA missions. It is operated out of the NASA Johnson Space Center.

The reduced gravity environment is achieved by flying a series of parabolic maneuvers. This results in short periods of less than one "G" acceleration. The lengths of these reduced gravity periods depends on the "G" level required for the specific test, usually 15 seconds to 40 seconds. These maneuvers could be flown consecutively or separated by enough time to alter the test setup. Each parabola is initiated with a 1.9G pull-up and concluded with a 1.8G pull-out. Normal missions last about two hours and consist of 40 parabolic maneuvers. All parabolic flights are flown from Ellington Field.

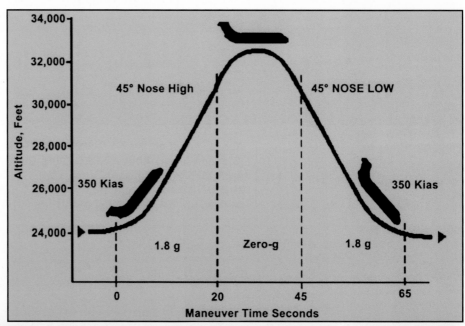

FLY 1/144 SCALE C-9B SKYTRAIN II MODEL KIT NUMBER 14403

Starting in 2009, Fly produced a large line of DC-9/C-9 model kits in 1/144 scale. Four of these kits represented military contracted aircraft. Kit # 14401 models the Firebird II test ship operated by government and later Raytheon; kit # 14002 depicted NASA's "Vomit Comet", BuNo 162754, NASA N932NA; kit # 14403 depicted a C-9B, BuNo 164607 RX/607 from VR-57, and kit # 14005 a USAF VC-9C. The C-9B kit included 41 white plastic parts.

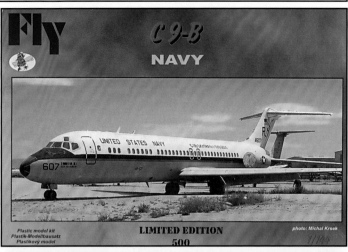

HASEGAWA 1/200 SCALE C-9B SKYTRAIN II KIT
GARTEX 1/200 SCALE C-9A NIGHTINGALE MODEL KIT

Hasegawa had issued a number of DC-9 airliner kits in their 1/200 scale series. In 1997, Gartex released kit # GA14, a C-9A Nightingale kit that included all the Hasegawa plastic parts (twenty grey plastic pieces) except the fuselage. A replacement one-piece resin fuselage was included. Excellent decals for the 374th TAW C-9As S/N 67-22583 (20th AAS) and 71-0874 (30th AAS) were included.

Also in 1997, Hasegawa releaed a C-9B Skytrain II as kit # 51907/SP207. It too included a one-piece resin fuselage along with its plastic parts. Decals provided markings for a VR-59 "Lone Star Express" Skytrain II, BuNo 161266 RY/266.

Both kits included a three-piece smoked clear plastic display stand.

C-9B SKYTRAIN II 'U.S. NAVY'

GA:14

1:200 Scale C-9A NIGHTINGALE

94

C-9B CARRIER ONBOARD DELIVERY (COD) / TANKER PROPOSAL

In 1972, McDonnell Douglas proposed to the Navy a COD aircraft based on a short fuselage (104.4 ft) DC-9-20. It would have retained the C-9B's cargo door and could be configured as follows: one pallet, forty seats; two pallets, twenty seats; two F-14 engines, twenty seats; three pallets, fifteen seats and eight litters, twenty seats. Estimated empty weight was 55,537 lbs, maximun take-off weight 98,400 lbs and maximum landing weight of 75,000 lbs. Range with a 10,000 lb payload was estimated at 2,700 miles in clear weather.

It would have been capable of operating off of the Midway class carriers and up. Without folding outer wing panels, two could be spotted on the deck of a CVA-41 class ship without hindering normal carrier operations and three on the super carriers. However, folding outer wing panels were also proposed to improve spotting.

The DC-9 was designed to operate from moderate to short runways in commercial service. Therefore, it has the basic flying qualities necessary for carrier operations: low approach speed (114 knots), outstanding speed stability on the glideslope, lateral-directional stability, control harmony, fast climb response in waveoff, and excellent pilot visibility. The C-9 (COD) retains all of these basic qualities, while incorporating nose gear catapult tow and a new long-stroke landing gear designed for high sink speeds. For catapulting, the nose

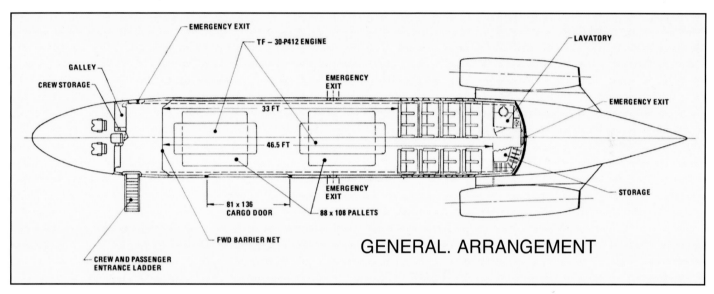

GENERAL. ARRANGEMENT

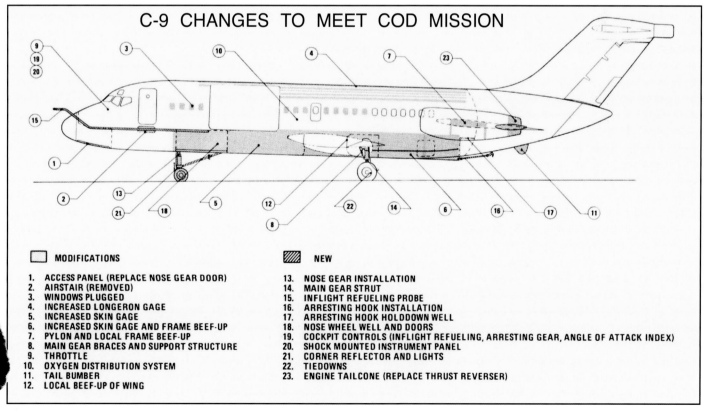

C-9 CHANGES TO MEET COD MISSION

☐ MODIFICATIONS	▨ NEW
1. ACCESS PANEL (REPLACE NOSE GEAR DOOR)	13. NOSE GEAR INSTALLATION
2. AIRSTAIR (REMOVED)	14. MAIN GEAR STRUT
3. WINDOWS PLUGGED	15. INFLIGHT REFUELING PROBE
4. INCREASED LONGERON GAGE	16. ARRESTING HOOK INSTALLATION
5. INCREASED SKIN GAGE	17. ARRESTING HOOK HOLDDOWN WELL
6. INCREASED SKIN GAGE AND FRAME BEEF-UP	18. NOSE WHEEL WELL AND DOORS
7. PYLON AND LOCAL FRAME BEEF-UP	19. COCKPIT CONTROLS (INFLIGHT REFUELING, ARRESTING GEAR, ANGLE OF ATTACK INDEX)
8. MAIN GEAR BRACES AND SUPPORT STRUCTURE	20. SHOCK MOUNTED INSTRUMENT PANEL
9. THROTTLE	21. CORNER REFLECTOR AND LIGHTS
10. OXYGEN DISTRIBUTION SYSTEM	22. TIEDOWNS
11. TAIL BUMBER	23. ENGINE TAILCONE (REPLACE THRUST REVERSER)
12. LOCAL BEEF-UP OF WING	

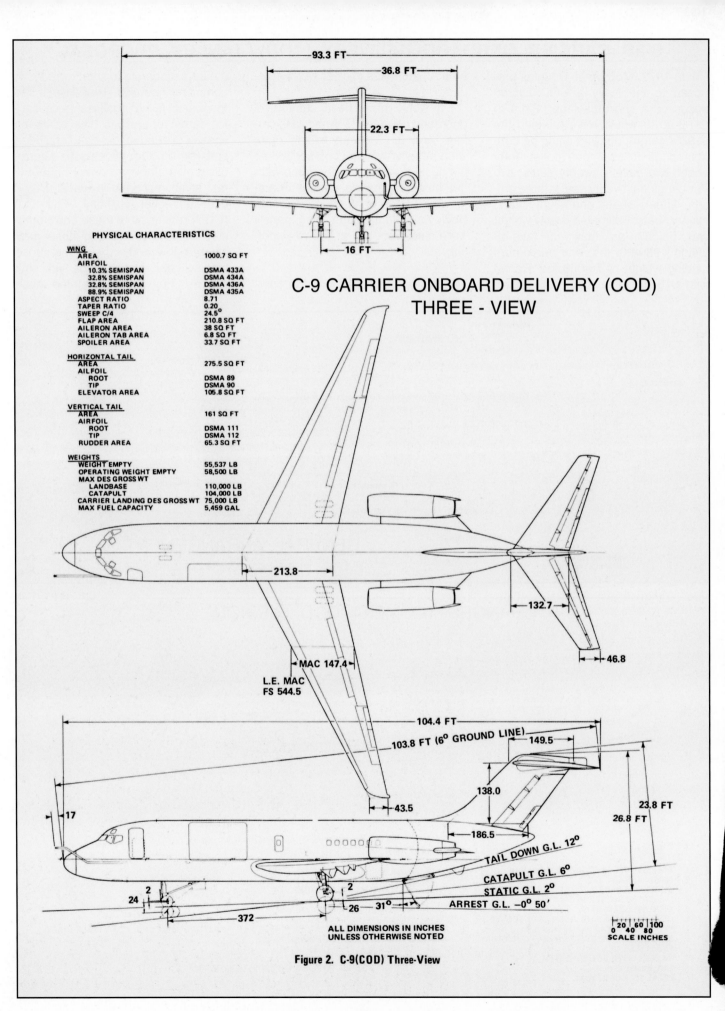

C-9 CARRIER ONBOARD DELIVERY (COD) THREE - VIEW

PHYSICAL CHARACTERISTICS

WING
AREA	1000.7 SQ FT
AIRFOIL	
10.3% SEMISPAN	DSMA 433A
32.8% SEMISPAN	DSMA 434A
32.8% SEMISPAN	DSMA 436A
88.9% SEMISPAN	DSMA 435A
ASPECT RATIO	8.71
TAPER RATIO	0.20
SWEEP C/4	24.5°
FLAP AREA	210.8 SQ FT
AILERON AREA	38 SQ FT
AILERON TAB AREA	6.8 SQ FT
SPOILER AREA	33.7 SQ FT

HORIZONTAL TAIL
AREA	275.5 SQ FT
AILFOIL	
ROOT	DSMA 89
TIP	DSMA 90
ELEVATOR AREA	105.8 SQ FT

VERTICAL TAIL
AREA	161 SQ FT
AIRFOIL	
ROOT	DSMA 111
TIP	DSMA 112
RUDDER AREA	65.3 SQ FT

WEIGHTS
WEIGHT EMPTY	55,537 LB
OPERATING WEIGHT EMPTY	58,500 LB
MAX DES GROSS WT	
LANDBASE	110,000 LB
CATAPULT	104,000 LB
CARRIER LANDING DES GROSS WT	75,000 LB
MAX FUEL CAPACITY	5,459 GAL

ALL DIMENSIONS IN INCHES
UNLESS OTHERWISE NOTED

Figure 2. C-9(COD) Three-View

gear is extended to give a 6-degree nose-up attitude. As a result, little rotation is required off the bow, ideal for catapulting at night or in obscured visibility.

Additionally, a refueling/tanker kit was proposed using D-704 buddy stores. Because of the commonality with the C-9B, this kit would have been usable on the C-9B too.

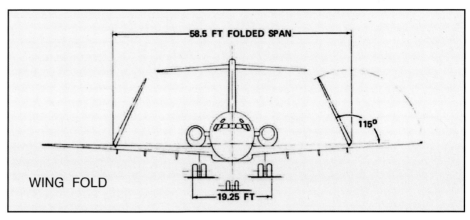

WING FOLD

58.5 FT FOLDED SPAN

115°

19.25 FT

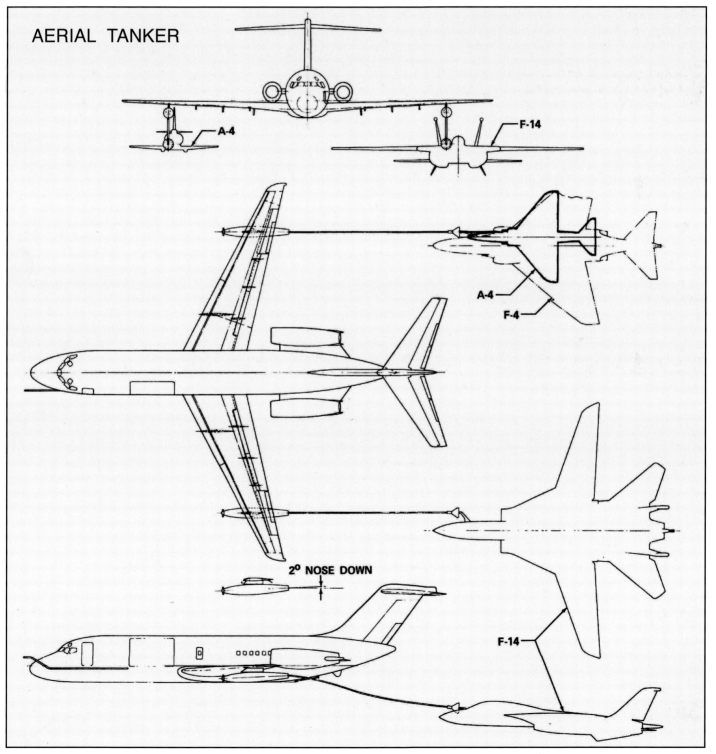

AERIAL TANKER

A-4

F-14

A-4

F-4

F-14

2° NOSE DOWN